WE TAKE YOUR CONTRACTOR BUSINESS NEXT LEVEL

MW00889643

SOUTH CAROLINA

1 CONTRACTOR CLUB

The #1 Contractor Service Provider

South Carolina's #1 contracting school for over 15 years now offers expanded contractor services.

1 EXAM PREP
AMERICA'S #1 CONTRACTOR SCHOOL

Contractor Exam Prep

- ⊘ Live Virtual Classes
- ⊘ Online Courses & Tutoring
- ⊘ Exam Book Rental
- ⊘ Application Assistance

USE CODE **CLUB24**
FOR 10% OFF!

1 INSURANCE SOLUTIONS
AMERICA'S #1 CONTRACTOR INSURANCE

Contractor Insurance

- ⊘ General Liability Insurance
- ⊘ Builder's Risk Insurance
- ⊘ Workers' Compensation
- ⊘ Life & Health Insurance

Scan Now
Get a Free Quote!

1 CONTRACTOR SOLUTIONS
AMERICA'S #1 CONTRACTOR SERVICES PROVIDER

Contractor Permits

- ⊘ Permit Expediters
- ⊘ General Trade Permits
- ⊘ License Registration
- ⊘ NOC Recording

USE CODE **PERMIT24**
50% OFF Your First Permit!

1ExamPrep.com
(877) 775-9400

1InsuranceSolutions.com
(877) 700-0243

1ContractorSolutions.com
(877) 702-5377

Author: One Exam Prep (1-877-804-3959)
www.1examprep.com

VISIT US HERE FOR EXCLUSIVE OFFERS

Unleashing the Power Of Digital Marketing For Your Contractor Business

- Company Branding
- Contractor Website
- Social Media Templates
- 1-on-1 Marketing Consultations
- Google Search Optimazation

WWW.154AGENCY.COM

TABLE OF CONTENTS

SC Residential Contractor Requirements

A contractors license is required in South Carolina for any residential work that exceeds over $5,000 in value and for residential specialty work over $200.

The **first step** in the licensing process is to gain pre-approval by **submitting an application** to the Residential Builders Commission documenting the following:

1. **Experience:** Documentation of one (1) year of Commission-approved experience under the supervision of a licensee in the trade in which you are applying.
2. **Financial information:** financial statement or surety bond.

An application fee of $100 must be sent with the application when seeking pre-approval.

Once approved, you may take the necessary exams. All Residential Contractor candidates are required to pass two (2) open book exams:

1. Business Management and Law examination
2. Technical (trade) examination of the specific license subcategory that you are applying for.

The fee for the exam is $90.00.

The licensing fee for the Residential Builder is $80 for 12 months or less and $160 for 12 months or more. The licensing fee is due after passing the exams.

Scope of Work - SC Residential Builder

This Residential Bulder examination is limited to construction, remodeling, repair and improvement of one-, two-, or multi-family residences not exceeding three stories in height and/or 16 units in any single apartment building.

Testing Company Information

The Residential Builder Exam is administered by PSI. PSI has examination centers in many regions across the United States.

For all state specific information please visit - PSI Exam License Page

1. Select Jurisdiction - South Carolina
2. Select SC Residential Contractors
3. Select Your License Classification

Examination Outline

The Residential Builder examination is an open book exam composed of 110 questions. You will have 360 minutes to complete the exam and must answer 77 correct (70%) in order to pass.

Total Questions:	110
Time Limit:	6 hours
Correct Required to Pass:	77 (70 %)

Subjects	No. of Items
General Building Construction	74
Residential Electrical	12
Residential HVAC	12
Residential Plumbing	12
Total Questions: 110	

Approved References

Candidates may bring reference book(s) listed below into the exam. These reference materials were used to prepare the questions for this examination.

1. International Residential Code for One- and Two-Family Dwellings, 2018 or 2021 Edition
   Effective 9/1/23 only the 2021 can be used
2. Carpentry and Building Construction 2010 or 2016
3. The Contractor's Guide to Quality Concrete Construction, 3rd Edition
4. Modern Masonry - Brick, Block, Stone, Clois E. Kicklighter, 8th Edition (2015)
5. BCSI: Guide to Good Practice for Handling, Installing, Restraining, and Bracing of Metal Plate Connected Wood Trusses, 2013
6. Gypsum Construction Handbook, 7th Ed., 2014

Important Notes

Reference books may be highlighted and/or indexed. They must be otherwise unmarked (not written in) and may not contain additional papers (loose or attached). **Proctors will thoroughly inspect all books before and after your examination.**

References may be tabbed/indexed with permanent tabs only. (Permanent tabs are defined as tabs that would tear the page if removed). Temporary tabs, (defined as Post-It Notes) or other tabs that may be removed without tearing the page) are not allowed and must be removed from the reference before the exam will begin.

The list of acceptable tabs below is a guide only and does not guarantee that you will be able to use them. However, if they are applied correctly, these tabs will stick onto pages and will tear the page if you try to remove them. This is only a sample list

Acceptable Tabs

- Avery Swift Tabs Self-Adhesive Permanent Plastic Tabs
- Redi-Tag Self-Stick Permanent Adhesive Index Tabs

Unacceptable Tabs

- Post-It Index Flags
- Post-It Flags

NO MATTER WHAT IS ON THE TAB PACKAGE, IF THE PSI PROCTOR IS ABLE TO REMOVE THE TABS WITHOUT RIPPING THE PAGE, YOU WILL NEED TO REMOVE THE TABS BEFORE YOU TAKE THE EXAM. DO NOT USE THE TABS THAT HAVE PAPER INSERTS. THE PAPER INSERTS WILL BE REMOVED.

- Candidates may use a silent, non-printing, non-programmable calculator in the examination center. Candidates will also be provided with a magnifying glass upon request.
- Please note that a "Ruler" or "Scale" is not required for these examinations.

Scheduling Your Exam

Individuals wishing to sit for the examination **must first submit an application** with the South Carolina Residential Builders Commission for review/approval. The Commission will notify the applicant and PSI once an applicant has been approved to take the examination.

SCHEDULE EXAMS ON-LINE

For the fastest and most convenient examination scheduling process, PSI recommends that you register for your examinations using the Internet. You register online by accessing PSI's registration website at https://test-takers.psiexams.com/scrb. Internet registration is available 24 hours a day. Log onto PSI's website and select Sign in / Create Account. Select Create Account. You are now ready to pay and schedule for the exam. Enter your zip code and a list of the testing sites closest to you will appear. Once you select the desired test site, available dates will appear.

SCHEDULE EXAMS BY TELEPHONE

For telephone registration, you will need a valid credit card (Visa, MasterCard, American Express or Discover). PSI registrars are available at (855) 340-3701, Monday through Friday between 7:30 am and 10:00 pm, and Saturday-Sunday between 9:00 am and 5:30 pm, Eastern Time, to receive your payment and schedule your appointment for the examination.

Additional Information

For Additional Information please see the South Carolina Residential Contractor Candidate Information Bulletin

STRATEGY FOR TEST TAKING

The preparation for an exam starts at the beginning of the course. It is essential to have the subject's program, become aware of the program, know it, review the books and support materials, and attend classes or tutoring sessions. The greater the time invested in preparing for your exam,the more likely you will pass it the first time around. The exam is just the first goal of a long career.

Prepare Mentally and Physically

Preparing for the exams depends, to a large extent, on the way you study. But other factors directly influence your academic performance, such as diet and exercise. Although the idea is to maintain a healthy and balanced diet throughout the year and exercise regularly, it is even more essential when preparing for your exams.

It is about eating breakfast that gives us the energy to face the day and supply the brain with enough glucose to get the most out of our study hours. Hydrating correctly for the day with water, dividing meals into five or six, and not overdoing it with caffeine will enhance our ability to pay attention and improve memory.

The same thing happens with exercise: Exercising will help us remove stress, rest better, and wake up feeling refreshed and more alert. Regular exercise also improves learning on two levels: it boosts cognitive function and memory retention. The more oxygenated nutrients the brain gets, the better it can perform, especially during exams.

Study planning: The first step to successfully passing the exams is planning well. This involves studying the subjects or content areas that will be on the exam daily. As the day of the exam approaches, we will only have to do an in-depth review of the entire exam scope to reach the exam date with all the suitably prepared subjects.

Reading: It is the general way to get in touch with a topic. When reading the scope of the exam, we must identify different phases for reading comprehension. First, we must understand the text's ideas and then expose our doubts or convey to the instructor what we have not understood. After examining what we read, we will achieve a broad vision of the whole, and it will only be enough for us to look for the general ideas.

Highlighting the text: Highlighting will help us focus on the relevant information in the text, and later, will help us structure and organize for the actual exam. We will avoid overloading the text excessively with highlights, not to hinder the ability to find the right answers during the exam. Note: Most testing companies allow the references for open book exams to be highlighted and tabbed with permanently affixed tabs. Be sure to check with your State or Local Jurisdiction regarding your exam.

Organizational techniques: Organizing the study material is key to understanding the concepts that we have previously highlighted in the text. These techniques will help us clarify the subject's structure, order the ideas hierarchically, and shorten the text's length to facilitate review and active study.

Study sheets: Using study cards or flashcards may sound like a very old-fashioned technique, but it is quite an effective learning method for assimilating specific data. It is about making a 'mini summary' of an entire topic, which allows you to save a lot when creating them, and they are straightforward to consult.

Take Practice Tests: The practice tests are an excellent way to review before an exam; in addition to that, with these, you can check what you are failing and focus efforts where necessary. It is, without a doubt, one of the best study strategies.

How Can You Improve Your Exam Preparation?

Make sure:

- Study daily to make sure you understand the subject.
- Study each subject listed on the exam scope: highlight, make outlines, and summaries.
- When a topic is well learned, it is not easily forgotten. In studying the following topics, you will have to rely on the previous ones, serving as a review and consolidation.

- When the exam approaches, we have to review to anchor them more in memory.

How Can You Improve Taking the Exam?

- Losing the nerve before the exam: "nerves are useless and they are in the way of everything."
- Try to relax. Practice relaxation techniques.
- Do not try to check if you remember all the exam subjects; before the exam, your mind is in tension, you can no longer reinforce your memory, so concentrate on what you will do.
- Being physically and mentally fit: You must sleep well and get enough rest before the exam.
- Do not leave everything for the last moment; if you do, you give the memory time to settle the information it receives. The memory needs rest, and your memory will be more clear if there is order.

How Fully Understand the Exam Questions?

- Leave the nerves at home.
- Take your time to read the questions well. Read them all. Sometimes there may be more than one referring to the same topic, and you will have to decide the focus and content for each one.
- Before answering each particular question, read it several times until you make sure you understand it. Look for the keyword that tells you what to do: explain, demonstrate, define, calculate, find. If your exam is open book, look for keywords that will indicate which book to find the answer in — Practice Comprehensive Reading.
- After answering, reread the question and answers and double-check your selection.

How to Organize the Time You Have During the Exam?

- It is necessary to know each question's value since the same amount of time may not be devoted to each question or subject.
- Quick distribution of time is made. We must allow time for review.
- It would be best to start with the questions that you are familiar with and know the answers quickly. The best way to answer is by making, in the beginning, an outline that guides us during the exam.
- When there is no time to answer a question, don't leave the question not answered. It will be an automatic wrong answer rather than taking a 1 out of 4 chance of getting the answer correct.

How to Review and Correct the Exam?

- Before submitting the exam, you should review:

The content: Make sure that you have answered all the questions.

The form:

It is more than obvious to say that to pass any exam depends a lot on how you study, the time you dedicate, and the information retention capacity you have.

- However, it also requires taking into account many other factors, so the best we can do is use effective study techniques to help you pass that stressful exam.
- It is expected that as the exam approaches, nerves can begin to take over due to the lack of constant study. That is why it is essential to discover an ideal technique that will lead you to achieve success and pass.

Preparation to Examinations

As we previously mentioned, preparation for your exam starts at the beginning of the course. It is essential to have the subject's program, become aware of the program, know it, review the books and support materials, and attend classes or tutoring sessions. The more time invested in preparing for your exam, the more likely you will pass it the first time.

It is also essential to keep motivation high when studying and have a learning strategy for each subject. Above all, you should not fear exploring different study methods.

Conclusively, We Can Develop the Following Strategies

Method One:

You should not "jump" on the exam task immediately after you received it. It would also be best if you didn't go through the questions one at a time in their original order.

Observe the following procedure:

Read the directions very carefully. The exam instructions often contain valuable data. Always examine all guidelines carefully to make sure you understand what's being requested.

Take a deep breath, and then slowly scan your eyes throughout the exam to familiarize yourself with all the questions.

In the process, answer the questions to which you know the correct answer.

Tackle more difficult tasks, but don't spend too much time on them. Leave the most difficult questions for the end.

Your task is to give as many correct answers to questions that you are sure of. Scientists have proven that when you skim through the entire test, unresolved questions are already "looming" in your head even before seriously tackling its solution. This is very useful for a variety of reasons.

First, you subconsciously start thinking about a solution to the most challenging test questions.

Secondly, tests often come across questions containing hints and sometimes even a complete answer to other test questions.

In any case, before proceeding with the solution of exam tasks, first, review the questions and give answers where you can do it. Then start to puzzle over more complicated tasks.

Method Two:

Read each test question at least twice.

This is a handy tip because trick questions are widespread in tests. When we are in the exam, we want to solve the tasks as quickly as possible, as there is not enough time. Therefore, many students make a widespread mistake because they glimpse a question and immediately start sorting out the answers.

The fact is that test developers try to outwit the exam takers and dilute the standard tasks with tricky questions. Let's take a look at some of them:

In tests, you can often come across the following question: Which of the following does not contain "a," "b," or "c"? If you read the task inattentively, it is quite possible to quickly skip the "not" particle and give a wrong answer.

Other questions may contain several correct answers, and your task involves choosing the most correct one.

Summing up, you should not lose your vigilance since inattention often leads to mistakes. So, do not be lazy and reread the questions at least twice.

Method Three:

Double-check the answers right away, rather than postpone checking until the end.

The fact is that once you have answered the question, the information is still very fresh in your head. Therefore, by quickly checking your answers, you will significantly reduce the chances of accidentally missing one silly mistake. On the other hand, you will increase your chances of receiving a passing exam score.

However, this does not mean that you should not recheck your answers after solving all the tests. On the contrary, try to always leave some time for final checking. By adding this technique to your arsenal, you can undoubtedly increase the chance of getting a decent grade.

Method Four (for closed book exams):

If you come across a question, the answer to which you do not remember, or you feel that it literally "spins on the tongue" but does not come to mind, try to mentally transfer yourself to the place where you first heard about it.

There are 24 hours in a day. If 8 of them are spent sleeping, that gives you 16 hours to get some efficient and productive study done, right?

It seems simple enough. There are plenty of hours in a day, so why is it so hard to use this time effectively, especially around exam time?

We've found that managing their time effectively is one of the things that students struggle the most with around exam time. However, time management is also one of the things that schools never teach – how frustrating?!

In the weeks leading up to study leave, every teacher you have for every class you go to seems to pile on the work: Mrs Gibb from English class tells you that you have to prepare 3 practice essays for both your visual and written texts, your Geography teacher Miss Wood expects you to do every past exam paper for the last three years before the exam, Mr West your Maths teacher says that you have to finish all of the questions in that darned AME textbook if you want to do well on the exam.

But they expect you to do all of this without giving you any time management tips. Mrs Gibb, Miss Wood and Mr West all fail to tell you how it's humanly possible to complete all of this work without collapsing when you walk into the exam hall.

That's where we come in!

Read on for the time management tips that your teachers never gave you!

1. Focus on what you have to study – not what you don't.

It seems obvious, but think of all the times you've sat down to study and you've ended up spending 2 hours studying the concepts you already know like the back of your hand.

It's easier to study the subjects you like. Studying the concepts that you're already confident in is a lot less challenging than studying the concepts that you find the most difficult, as your brain will have to work less to learn this information.

Studying what you already know is a bad time management strategy because you'll leave all the important stuff to the last minute meaning you won't have the time to cover these concepts in depth.

The trouble with this tip is that it's often hard to decipher what you know and what you don't.

To figure out what you concepts you already know, and what concepts you still need to learn, complete a subject audit. A subject audit involves breaking down a particular subject into several points or sections and then analysing how well you know each of these points. You should spend most of your time studying those concepts that you have rated the most difficult. Find our study audit outline form here.

The key for effective time management is to review the easier material, but allow enough time to cover the harder concepts in depth so you're not left to study all of the most difficult concepts the night before the exam.

2. Work in sprints.

You may think that to have good time management skills you have to spend all of your time studying. However this is a misconception that many students hold.

Think of studying for exams like training for a marathon.

On your first day of training, you wouldn't go out and run 42kms. You would burn-out quickly due to a lack of prior training, and you would probably be put off running for a long time. This would not be a good way to manage your time. The better route to success would be to slowly work up to running the 42kms by running a bit further every day.

This simple idea of training in short bursts has been proven effective in all areas of human performance. You don't have to be a marathon runner to use this strategy!

When studying, you should start out small by studying in short, focused 'sprints' followed by brief breaks. Start by studying in 15 minute bursts followed by one 10 minute break. Over time, slowly increase the length of time you're studying (and breaking) for.

This strategy is effective because studying for short bursts promotes more intense focus, and will give your brain the time to process and consolidate information as opposed to studying for long periods of time which is not effective and may increase your chances of burnout.

Don't think of effective time management as studying for three hours straight with no breaks, think of effective time management as using your time wisely and in ways that will best promote retention of information.

Follow these steps to practice effective time management and become an expert studier (or marathon runner!) in no time:

1. **Set a timer for 15 minutes.**
2. **Put in some solid study until the timer goes off, making sure you're spending every minute working with no distractions.**
3. **Have a ten-minute break to check your phone, walk around, stretch, get outside etc.**
4. **Rinse and repeat.**
5. **Increase the amount of time you're studying for as you begin to feel more comfortable studying for extended lengths of time.**

3. Make a study system.

I'm sure you've been lectured by every teacher you've ever had to "make a study plan!!!" Study plans are effective for your time management, however they're sometimes hard to stick to.

Here at StudyTime, we find that the 'study system' is an effective strategy for really getting to the root of what you're studying. A study system is easier to stick to, and therefore fosters better time management skills, because it breaks tasks down into small chunks.

A study system is basically a simple list of steps that you can make to outline the steps you're going to take when you study. The list should start simple (4-5 things), but over time it should become more complex as you add steps to it.

Just like a workout plan at the gym or for sport, it will give you a clear direction of what action to take, making study much more efficient.

Over time, you can experiment with new study methods, and add them in to optimise the system.

Below is an example study formula that you could use when studying:

1. **Download the "Achievement Standard" from the NCEA website**
2. **Turn this into a checklist for what you already know and what you need to know**
3. **Break the checklist into main themes using a mind map**
4. **For each theme, make a summary sheet**
5. **After that, break down the key points of each summary and put these onto flash cards**
6. **Read through your notes and ensure you understand them, and then hit the flash cards**
7. **Test yourself on all of them first, then make two piles, one that's wrong and one that's right. Then redo the wrong pile again**
8. **Get someone else to test you**
9. **Practice exam papers – test yourself using exam papers from the past 2-3 years and time yourself**
10. **Work through the answers**
11. **Write a sheet of all tips/tricks i.e. things you got wrong in the practice exam papers**
12. **Redo exam paper and make model answers**
13. **Adjust flashcards if necessary i.e. make new ones based on the exam papers**
14. **Re-test all your flashcards**

Creating a study system will keep you on track and it will allow you to effectively plan out your time while studying.

4. Practice distributed learning.

Imagine your Maths teacher gave you seven equations to do for homework. How would you answer these questions? Would you do one question per day for seven days, or would you do all seven questions in one day?

You may think that it would be a better time management strategy to do all seven questions at once and get them over and done with. However, this is an ineffective way to manage your time.

The brain works better when it has time to process information. Neuroscience has shown that your brain needs time to consolidate information that has been newly learned, in order to form strong links between neurons and thus strong memories.

If the learning is done in one big chunk, you'll just forget it after three days. However, if you review it a day after, then you'll retain it for seven days.

When making a study schedule, you should space out when you study for each subject. For example, don't spend one day studying English, then the next day studying Maths, then the next day studying Biology. Instead, you should alternate studying for these subjects throughout the day. Do one hour of Maths, then one hour of English study, then one hour of Biology, and so on.

This is a much better way to manage your time, because the more often you review a concept, the more solidified it will be in your mind. This is because there will be more time to consolidate this into your memory. Also, taking breaks between reviewing certain concepts will give your brain time to process the information.

Try it out!

International Residential Code 2021
Tabs and Highlights

These 1 Exam Prep Tabs are based on *International Residential Code, 2021 Edition.*

Each Tabs sheet has five rows of tabs. Start with the first tab at the first row at the top of the page and proceed down that row placing the tabs at the locations listed below. Place each tab in your book setting it down one notch until you get to the bottom of the page, and then start back at the top again. After you have completed tabbing your book (the last tab is usually the glossary, appendix, or index), then you may start highlighting your book.

*** *This concludes the tabs for this book. Please continue with the highlights on the following page.* ***

ABC 08/19/2021

Section #	Highlight
R101.2	**Scope.** The provisions of this code shall apply to the construction, *alteration*, movement enlargement, replacement, *repair*, equipment, use and occupancy, location, removal and demolition of detached one- and two- family dwellings and *townhouses* not more than three stories above *grade plane* in height with a separate means of egress and their *accessory structures* not more than three stories above *grade plane* in height.
R102.1	**General.** Where there is a conflict between a general requirement and a specific requirement, the specific requirement shall be applicable. Where, in any specific case, different sections of this code specify different materials, methods of construction or other requirements, the most restrictive shall govern.
R105.2	**Work exempt from permit.** *Permits* shall not be required for the following: Building (Highlight 1 – 10)
R105.5	**Expiration:** Every *permit* issued shall become invalid unless the work is authorized by such *permit* is commenced within 180 days after its issuance or after commencement of work if more than 180 days pass between inspections.
R105.7	**Placement of permit.** The building *permit* or a copy shall be kept on the site of the work until completion of the project.
R106.3.1	**Approval of construction documents.** Where the *building official* issues a *permit*, the *construction documents* shall be *approved* in writing or by a stamp that states "REVIEWED FOR CODE COMPLIANCE." One set of *documents* so reviewed shall be retained by the *building official*. The other set shall be returned to the applicant, shall be kept at the site of work and shall be open to inspection by the *building official* or a duly authorized representative.
R107.1	**General:** Such *permits* shall be limited as to time of service, but not be permitted for more than 180 days.
R109.4	**Approval required.** Work shall not be done beyond the point indicated in each successive inspection without first obtaining the approval of the *building official*. The *building official* upon notification, shall make the requested inspections and shall either indicate the portion of the construction that is satisfactory as completed, or shall notify the permit holder or an agent of the permit holder wherein the same fails to comply with this code. Any portions that do not comply shall be corrected and such portion shall not be covered or concealed until authorized by the *building official*.
R111.2	**Temporary connection.** The *building official* shall have the authority to authorize the temporary connection of the building or system to the utility, source of energy, fuel or power.
R114.1	**Authority.** Where the building official finds any work regulated by this code being performed in a manner contrary to the provisions of this code or in a dangerous or unsafe manner, the building official is authorized to issue a stop work order.
R202	**Definitions:**
	▪ **[RB] Basement**
	▪ **[RB] Building Line**
	▪ **[RB] Dalle Glass**
	▪ **[RB] Dead Loads**
	▪ **[RB] Dwelling**
	▪ **[RB] Dwelling Unit**
	▪ **[RB] Live Loads**

Section #	Highlight

R301.1 — **Application.** Buildings and structures, and parts thereof, shall be constructed to safely support all loads, including dead loads, live loads, roof loads, flood loads, snow loads, wind loads and seismic loads as prescribed by this code.

R301.1.3 — **Engineered design.** Where a building of otherwise conventional construction contains structural elements exceeding the limits of Section R301 or otherwise not conforming to this code, these elements shall be designed in accordance with accepted engineering practice.

R301.2.1.2 — **Protection of openings.** Glazed opening protection for windborne debris shall meet the requirements of the Large Missile Test of ASTM E1886 and ASTM E1996 as modified in Section 301.2.1.2.1.

Exception: *Wood structural panels* with a thickness of not less than 7/16 inch (11 mm) and a span of not more than 8 feet (2438 mm) shall be permitted for opening protection.

Attachment in accordance with Table R301.2.1.2 is permitted for buildings with a mean roof height of 45 feet (13,728 mm) or less where the ultimate design wind speed, V_{ult}, is 180 mph (290 kph) or less.

Figure R301.1(1) — **Weathering Probability Map for Concrete[a,b]**

Figure R301.2(2) — **Ultimate Design Wind Speeds**

R301.2.1.3 — **Wind speed conversion.** the ultimate design wind speeds, V_{ult}, of Figure R301.2(2) shall be converted to nominal design wind speeds, V_{asd}, using Table R301.2.1.3.

Table R301.2.1.2 — **Windborne Debris Protection Fastening Schedule for Wood Structural Panels[a,b,c,d]**

Table R301.2.1.3 — **Wind Speed Conversions[a]**

Table R301.6 — **Minimum Roof Live Loads in Pounds-Force Per Square Foot of Horizontal Projection**

R310.1 — **Emergency escape and rescue opening required.** *Basements, habitable attics* and every sleeping room shall have not less than one operable *emergency escape and rescue opening.* Where *basements* contain one or more sleeping rooms, an *emergency escape* and *rescue opening* shall be required in each sleeping room. *Emergency escape and rescue openings* shall open directly into a *public* way, or to a *yard* or court having a minimum width of 36 inches (914 mm) that opens to a public way.

R310.2.1 — **Minimum opening size.** Emergency escape and rescue openings shall have a net clear opening of not less than 5.7 square feet (0.530 m^2).

R310.2.3 — **Maximum height from floor.** Emergency escape and rescue openings shall have the bottom of the clear opening not greater than 44 inches (118 mm) above the floor.

R310.4.1 — **Minimum size.** The horizontal area of the area well shall be not less than 9 square feet (0.9 m^2), with a horizontal projection and width of not less than 36 inches (914 mm).

Figure R318.4 — **Termite Infestation Probability Map**

Section #	Highlight
R401.3	**Drainage.** Surface drainage shall be diverted to a storm sewer conveyance or other *approved* point of collection that does not create a hazard. *Lots* shall be graded to drain surface water away from foundation walls. The *grade* shall fall a minimum of 6 inches (152 mm) within the first 10 feet (3048 mm).
R401.4	**Soil tests.** Where quantifiable data created by accepted soil science methodologies indicate *expansive soils, compressible soils,* shifting soils or other questionable soil characteristics are likely to be present, the building official shall determine whether to require a soil test to determine the soil's characteristics at a particular location. This test shall be done by an *approved agency* using an *approved* method.
Table R401.4.1	**Presumptive Load-Bearing Values of Foundation Materials[a]**
R402.1	**Wood foundations.** Wood foundation systems shall be designed and installed in accordance with the provisions of this code.
R402.1.1	**Fasteners:** Fasteners used below *grade* to attach plywood to the exterior side of exterior *basement* or crawl-space wall studs, or fasteners used in knee wall construction shall be of... Electro-galvanized steel nails and galvanized (zinc coated) steel staples shall not be permitted.
R402.1.2	**Wood treatment.** Where lumber or plywood is cut or drilled after treatment, the treated surface shall be field treated with copper naphthenate, the concentration of which shall contain not less than 2-percent copper metal, by repeated brushing, dipping or soaking until the wood cannot absorb more preservative.
R402.2	**Concrete.** Concrete shall have a minimum specified compressive strength of f'_c, as shown in Table R402.2. Concrete subject...Materials used to produce concrete and testing thereof shall comply with the applicable standards listed in Chapter 19 and 20 of ACI 318 or ACI 332.
R403.1.1	**Minimum size.** The minimum width, W, and thickness, T, for concrete footings shall be in accordance with Tables R403.1(1) through R403.1(3) and Figure R403.1(1) or R403.1.3, as applicable, but not less than 12 inches (305 mm) in width and 6 inches (152 mm) in depth. Footings for wood foundations shall be in accordance with the details set forth in Section R403.2, and Figures R403.1(2) and R403.1(3). Footings for precast foundations shall be in accordance with the details set forth in Section R403.4, Table R403.4, and Figures R403.4(1) and R403.4(2).
Table R402.2	**Minimum Specified Compressive Strength of Concrete**
Table R403.1(1)	**Minimum Width and Thickness for Concrete Footings for Light-Frame Construction**
Figure R403.1(2)	**Permanent Wood Foundation Basement Wall Section**
Figure R403.1(3)	**Permanent Wood Foundation Crawl Space Section**
R403.1.4	**Minimum depth.** Exterior footings shall be placed not less than 12 inches (305 mm) below the undisturbed ground surface.
R403.1.7.3	**Foundation elevation.** On graded sites, the top of any exterior foundation shall extend above the elevation of the street that are at point of discharge or the inlet of an *approved* drainage device not less than 12 inches (305 mm) plus 2 percent.
R404.1.5	**Foundation wall thickness on walls supported**

Section #	Highlight
R404.1.5.1	**Masonry wall thickness.** Masonry foundation walls shall not be less than the thickness of the wall supported, except that masonry foundation walls of not less than 8-inch (203 mm) nominal thickness shall be permitted under brick veneered frame walls and under 10-inch-wide (254 mm) cavity walls where the total height of the wall supported, including gables, is not more than 20 feet (6096 mm), provided that the requirements of Section R404.1.1 are met.
R404.1.6	**Height above finished grade.** Concrete and masonry foundation walls shall extend above the finished *grade* adjacent to the foundation at all points not less 4 inches (102 mm) were masonry veneer is used and a minimum of 6 inches (152 mm) elsewhere.
R404.1.8	**Rubble stone masonry.** Rubble stone masonry foundation walls shall have a minimum thickness 16 inches (406 mm), shall not support an unbalanced backfill exceeding 8 feet (2438 mm) in height, shall not support a soil pressure greater than 30 pounds per square foot per foot (4.71 kPa/m).
R404.3	**Wood sill plates.** Wood sill plates shall be not less than 2-inch by 4-inch (51 mm by 102 mm) nominal lumber. Sill plate anchorage shall be in accordance with Sections R403.1.6 and R602.11.
R405.1	**Concrete or masonry foundations.** Drains shall be provided around concrete or masonry foundations that retain earth and enclose habitable or usable spaces located below *grade*. Gravel or crushed store drains shall extend at least 1 foot (305 mm) beyond the outside edge of the footing and 6 inches (152 mm) above the top of the footing and covered with an *approved* filter membrane material. Drainage tiles or perforated pipe shall be placed on not less than 2 inches (51 mm) of washed gravel or crushed rock not less than one sieve size larger than the tile joint opening or perforation and covered with not less than 6 inches (152 mm) of the same material.
R406.2	**Concrete and masonry foundation waterproofing.** In areas where high water table or other severe soil water conditions are known to exist, exterior foundation walls that retain… Walls shall be waterproofed in accordance with one of the following: (Highlight 1 – 6) **Exception:** Use of plastic roofing cements, acrylic coatings, latex coatings, mortars and pargings to seal ICF walls is permitted.
R407.3	**Structural requirements.** Wood columns shall not be less in nominal size than 4 inches by 4 inches (102 mm by 102 mm). Steel columns shall be not less than 3-inch-diameter (76 mm) Schedule 40 pipe manufactured in accordance with ASTM A53/A53M Grade B or *approved* equivalent.
R408.1	**Moisture control.** The under-floor space between the bottom of the floor joists and the earth under any building (except space occupied by a basement) shall comply with Section R408.2 or R408.3.
R408.2	**Openings for under-floor ventilation.** Ventilation openings shall be covered for their height and width with any of the following materials provided that the least dimension of the covering shall not exceed 1/4 inch (6.4 mm), and operational louvers are permitted: (Highlight 1 – 6)
R408.4	**Access.** Access shall be provided for all under- floor spaces. Access openings through the floor shall be not smaller than 18 inches by 24 inches (457 mm by 610 mm). Openings… Through wall access openings shall not be located under a door to the residence.

Section #	Highlight
R502.2.2	**Blocking and subflooring.** Blocking for fastening panel edges or fixtures shall be not less than utility grade lumber…Fireblocking shall be of any grade of lumber.
R502.11	**Wood trusses**
R502.11.1	**Design.** The *truss design drawings* shall be prepared…in accordance with Section R106.1.
R502.11.2	**Bracing.** Trusses shall be braced to prevent rotation…on individual *truss design drawings*.
R502.11.3	**Alterations to trusses.** *Alterations* resulting in the addition of load that exceeds the design load for the truss, shall not be permitted without verification that the truss is capable of supporting the additional load.
R502.11.4	**Truss design drawings.** *Truss design drawings* shall include, at a minimum, the information specified below: (Highlight 1 – 12)
R502.13	**Fireblocking required.**
R503.1	**Lumber sheathing:** Maximum allowable spans for lumber used as floor sheathing shall conform to Tables R503.1, R503.2.1.1(1) and R503.2.1.1(2).
Table R503.1	**Minimum Thickness of Lumber Floor Sheathing**
R503.2	**Wood structural panel sheathing**
Table R503.2.1.1(1)	**Allowable Spans and Loads For Wood Structural Panels For Roof And Subfloor Sheathing And Combination Subfloor Underlayment[a,b,c]**
Table R503.2.1.1(2)	**Allowable Spans for Sanded Plywood Combination Subfloor Underlayment[a]**
R503.2.2	**Allowable spans.** The maximum allowable span for *wood structural panels* used as subfloor or combination subfloor underlayment shall be set forth in Table R503.2.1.1(1), or APA E30.
R503.2.3	**Installation.** *Wood structural panels* used as subfloor or combination subfloor or combination subfloor underlayment shall be attached to wood framing in accordance with R602.3(1) and shall be attached to cold-formed steel framing in accordance with Table R505.3.1(2).
R504.1.3	**Uplift and buckling.** Where required, resistance shall be provided to uplift or restraint against buckling shall be provided by interior bearing walls or properly designed stub walls anchored in the supporting soil below.
R504.2	**Site preparation.** The area within the foundation walls shall have all vegetation, topsoil and foreign material removed, and any fill material that is added shall be free of vegetation and foreign material. The fill shall be compacted to ensure uniform support of the pressure preservative treated-wood floor sleepers.
R504.2.1	**Base.** A minimum 4-inch-thick (102 mm) granular base gravel maximum size ¾ inch (19.1 mm) or crushed stone having a maximum size of ½ inch (12.7 mm) shall be placed on compacted earth.
R504.2.2	**Moisture barrier.** Polyethylene sheeting of minimum 6-mil (0.15 mm) thickness shall be placed over the granular base. Joints shall be lapped 6 inches (152 mm) and left unsealed.
R506.1	**General.** Floors shall be a minimum 3½ inches (89 mm) thick (for *expansive soils*, see Section R403.1.8).

Section #	Highlight
R506.2	**Site preparation.** The area within the foundation walls shall have all vegetation, top soil and foreign material removed.
R506.2.1	**Fill.** Fill material shall be free of vegetation and foreign material. The fill shall be compacted to ensure uniform support of the slab, and except where approved, the fill depths shall not exceed 24 inches (610 mm) for clean sand or gravel and 8 inches (203 mm) for earth.
R506.2.2	**Base.** A 4-inch-thick (102 mm) base course consisting of clean grated sand, gravel, crushed stone, crushed concrete or crushed blast-furnace slag passing a 2-inch (51 mm) sieve shall be placed on the prepared subgrade when the slab is below *grade*.

Exception: A base course is not required when the slab is installed on well-drained or sand-gravel mixture soils classified as Group I according to the United Soil Classification System in accordance with Table R405.1.

R506.2.3	**Vapor retarder.** A minimum 10-mil (0.010 inch; 0.254 mm) vapor retarder conforming to ASTM E1745 Class A requirements with joints lapped not less than 6 inches (152 mm) shall be placed between the concrete floor slab and the base course or the prepared subgrade where a base course does not exist.
Table R602.3(1)	**Fastening Schedule**
R602.6	**Drilling and notching of studs.**

    1. Notching
    2. Boring

Figure R602.6(1)	**Notching And Bored Hole Limitations For Exterior Walls And Bearing Walls**
Figure R602.6(2)	**Notching And Bored Hole Limitations For Interior Nonbearing Walls**
R602.6.1	**Drilling and notching of top plate.** Where piping or ductwork is placed in or partly in an exterior wall or interior *load-bearing wall*, necessitating cutting, drilling or notching of the… at each side or equivalent. The metal tie must extend not less than 6 inches past the opening.
Figure R602.6.1	**Top Plate Framing to Accommodate Piping**
R606.3.1	**Bed and head joints.** Unless otherwise required or indicated on the project drawings, head and bed joints shall be 3/8 inch thick (9.5 mm) thick, except that the thickness of the bed joint of the starting course placed over foundations shall be not less than ¼ inch (6.4 mm) and not more than ¾ inch (19.1 mm).
R606.5	**Corbeled masonry.** Corbeled masonry shall be in accordance with Sections R606.5.1 through R606.5.3.
R606.5.1	**Units:** *Solid masonry* or masonry units filled with mortar or grout shall be used for corbeling.
R606.5.2	**Corbel projection.** The maximum projection of one unit shall not exceed one-half the height of the unit or one-third the thickness at right angles to the wall. The maximum corbeled projection beyond the face of the wall shall not exceed: (Highlight 1 – 2)
R610.3	**Materials**

Section #	Highlight
R610.3.1	**Lumber.** The minimum lumber framing material used for SIPs prescribed in this document is NLGA graded No. 2 Spruce-pine-fir. Substitution of other wood species/grades that meet or exceed the mechanical properties and specific gravity of No. 2 Spruce-pine-fir shall be permitted.
R610.3.2	**SIP Screws.** Screws used for the erection of SIPs as specified in Section R610.5 shall be fabricated from steel, shall be provided by the SIP manufacturer…The screws shall be corrosion resistant and have a minimum shank diameter of 0.188 inch (4.7 mm) and a minimum head diameter of 0.620 inch (15.5 mm).
R610.3.3	**Nails.** Nails specified in Section R610 shall be common or galvanized box unless otherwise stated.
R701.1	**Application.** The provisions of this chapter shall control the design and construction of the interior and exterior wall coverings for buildings.
R702.1	**General.** Interior coverings or wall finishes shall be installed in accordance with this chapter and Table R702.1(1), R702.1.(2), R702.1(3) and R702.3.5. Interior…Interior finishes and materials shall conform to the flame spread and smoke-development of Section R302.9
Table R702.1(1)	**Thickness of Plaster**
Table R702.1(2)	**Gypsum Plaster Proportions[a]**
Table R702.1(3)	**Cement Plaster Proportions, Parts By Volume**
R702.2	**Interior plaster**
R702.2.3	**Support.** Support spacing for gypsum or metal lath on walls or ceilings shall not exceed 16 inches (406 mm) for 3/8-inch-thick (9.5 mm) or 24 inches (610 mm) for ½-inch-thick (12.7 mm) plain gypsum lath.
R702.3	**Gypsum board and gypsum panel products**
Table R702.3.5	**Minimum Thickness And Application of Gypsum Board And Gypsum Panel Products**
R702.3.5.1	**Screw fastening.** Screws for attaching gypsum board to wood framing shall be Type W or Type S in accordance with ASTM C1002 and shall penetrate the wood not less than 5/8 inch (15.9 mm).
R702.3.7	**Water-resistant gypsum backing board.** Water-resistant gypsum board shall not be installed over a Class I or II vapor retarder in a shower or tub compartment.
R702.5	**Other finishes.** Wood veneer paneling and hardboard paneling shall be placed on wood or cold-formed steel framing spaced not more than 16 inches (406 mm) on center…Wood veneer paneling not less than ¼-inch (6 mm) nominal thickness shall conform to ANSI/HPVA HP-1.
R703.2	**Water-resistive barrier.** Not fewer than one layer of *water-resistive barrier* shall be applied over studs or sheathing of all exterior walls with flashing as indicated in Section R703.4, in such a manner as to provide a continuous water-resistive barrier behind the exterior wall veneer.
	Water-resistive barrier materials shall comply with one of the following: (Highlight 1 – 4)
R703.5	**Wood, hardboard and wood structural panel siding**

Section #	Highlight
R703.5.2	**Panel siding.** Vertical joints in panel siding shall occur over framing…Horizontal joints in panel siding shall be lapped not less than 1 inch (25 mm) or shall be shiplapped or flashed with Z-flashing and occur over solid blocking, wood or wood structural panel sheathing.
R703.6	**Wood shakes and shingles**
Table R703.6.1	**Maximum Weather Exposure for Wood Shakes and Shingles on Exterior Walls**[a,b,c]
R703.6.3	**Attachment.** Each shake or shingle shall be held in place by two stainless steel Type 304, Type 316 or hot-dipped zinc-coated…The fasteners shall penetrate the sheathing or furring strips by not less than ½ inch (13 mm) and shall not be overdriven.
R703.8	**Anchored Stone and masonry veneer, general**
R703.8.6	**Weepholes.** Weepholes shall be provided in the outside wythe of masonry walls at a maximum spacing of 33 inches (838 mm) on center. Weepholes shall be not less than 3/16 inch (5 mm) in diameter. Weepholes shall be located immediately above the flashing.
R703.10	**Fiber cement siding**
R703.10.1	**Panel siding.** Panels shall be installed with the long dimension either parallel or perpendicular to framing. Vertical and horizontal joints shall occur over framing members and shall be protected with caulking, or with battens or flashing, or be vertical or horizontal shiplap, or otherwise designed to comply with Section R703.1.
R703.10.2	**Lap siding.** Fiber-cement lap siding having a maximum width of 12 inches (305 mm) shall comply with the requirements of ASTM C1186, Type A, minimum Grade II or ISO 8336, Category A, minimum Class 2. Lap siding shall be lapped a minimum of 1¼ inches (32 mm) and lap siding not having tongue-and-groove should have the ends protected with caulking.
R802.1.5.4	**Labeling.** The *label* shall contain: (Highlight 1 – 8)
R802.2	**Design and construction.** The roof and ceiling assembly shall provide continuous ties across the structure to prevent roof thrust from being applied to the supporting walls.
R802.4.2	**Framing details.** Rafters shall be framed opposite from each other to a ridge board, shall not be offset more than 11/2 inches (38 mm) from each other and shall be connected with a collar tie or ridge strap in accordance with Section R802.4.6 or directly opposite from each other to a gusset plate in accordance with Table R602.3(1).
Table R803.1	**Minimum Thickness of Lumber Roof Sheathing**
R806.1	**Ventilation required.** Ventilation openings shall have a least dimension of 1/16 inch (1.6 mm) minimum and 1/4 inch (6.4 mm) maximum. Ventilation openings having a least dimension larger than 1/4 inch (6.4 mm) shall be provided with corrosion-resistant wire cloth screening, perforated vinyl or similar with openings having a least dimension of 1/16 inch (1.6 mm) and 1/4 inch (6.4 mm) maximum.
R806.2	**Minimum vent area.** The minimum net free ventilating area shall be 1/150 of the area of the vented space.
R807.1	**Attic access.** Buildings with combustible ceiling or roof construction shall have an attic access opening to attic areas that have a vertical height of 30 inches (762 mm) or greater over an area of not less than 30 square feet (2.8 m^2).

Section #	Highlight

The rough-framed opening shall not be less than 22 inches by 30 inches (559 mm by 762 mm) and shall be located in a hallway or other location with *ready access.*

R902.1   **Roofing covering materials.** Class A, B or C roofing shall be installed in *jurisdictions* designated by law as requiring their use or where the edge of the roof is less than 3 feet (914 mm) from a *lot line.*

R903.2   **Flashing.** Flashings shall be installed in a manner that prevents moisture from entering the wall and roof through joints in copings, through moisture permeable materials and at intersections with parapet walls and other penetrations through the roof plane.

R903.2.1   **Locations.** Flashings shall be installed at wall and roof intersections, wherever there is a change in roof slope or direction and around roof openings.

R903.3   **Coping.** Parapet walls shall be properly coped with noncombustible, weatherproof materials of a width no less than the thickness of the parapet wall.

R903.4   **Roof drainage.** Unless roofs are sloped to drain over roof edges, roof drains shall be installed at each low point of the roof.

R903.4.1   **Secondary (emergency overflow) drains and scuppers.** Overflow drains having the same size as the roof drains shall be installed with the…shall be installed in the adjacent parapet walls with the inlet flow located 2 inches (51 mm) above the low point of the roof served.

905.1.1   **Underlayment.** *Underlayment* materials required to comply with ASTM D226, D1970, D4869 and D6757 shall bear a *label* indicating compliance to the standard designation and, if applicable, type classification indicated in Table R905.1.1(1).

Table R905.1.1(1)   **Underlayment Types**

R905.2   **Asphalt shingles**

R905.2.2   **Slope.** Asphalt shingles shall be used only on roof slopes of 2 units in 12 units horizontal …double *underlayment* application is required in accordance with section R905.1.1.

R905.2.5   **Fasteners.** Fasteners for asphalt shingles shall be galvanized, stainless, aluminum or copper roofing nails, minimum 12-gage [0.105 inch (3 mm)] shank with a minimum 3/8-inch-diameter (9.5 mm) head, complying with ASTM F1667, of a length to penetrate through the roofing materials and not less than 3/4 inch (19.1 mm) into the roof sheathing. Where the roof sheathing is less than 3/4 inch (19.1 mm) thick, the fasteners shall penetrate through the sheathing.

R905.2.6   **Attachment.** Asphalt shingles shall have the minimum number of fasteners required by the manufacturer's *approved* installation instructions, but not less than four fasteners per strip shingle or two fasteners per individual shingle. Where the roof slope exceeds 21 units vertical in 12 units horizontal (21:12, 175-percent slope), shingles shall be installed in accordance with the manufacturer's *approved* installation instructions.

R905.2.8.2   **Valleys.** Valley linings of the following types shall be permitted: (Highlight 1 – 3)

R905.2.8.5   **Drip edge.** Adjacent segments of drip edge shall be overlapped not less than 2 inches (51 mm) …deck not less than 2 inches (51 mm). Drip edges shall be mechanically fastened to the *roof deck* at not more than 12 inches (305 mm) o.c. with fasteners as specified in Section R905.2.5.

R905.3   **Clay and concrete tile**

Section #	Highlight
R905.3.5	**Concrete tile.** Concrete roof tile shall comply with ASTM C1492.
R905.3.6	**Fasteners.** Nails shall be corrosion resistant and not less than 11-gage[0.120 inch (3 mm)], 5/16-inch (11 mm) head, and of sufficient length to penetrate the deck not less than 3/4 inch (19 mm) or through the thickness of the deck, whichever is less.
R905.4	**Metal roof shingles**
R905.4.2	**Deck slope.** *Metal roof shingles* shall not be installed on roof slopes below 3 units vertical in 12 units horizontal (25-percent slope).
R905.4.6	**Flashing.** The valley flashing shall extend at least 8 inches (203 mm) from the centerline each way and shall have a splash diverter rib not less than 3/4 inch (19 mm) in height at…*underlayment* running the full length of the valley, in addition to *underlayment* required for *metal roof shingles.*
R905.6	**Slate shingles**
R905.6.3	**Underlayment.** *Underlayment* shall comply with Section R905.1.1.
Table R905.6.5	**Slate Shingle Headlap**
R905.6.6	**Flashing:** Valley flashing shall be not less than 15 inches (381 mm) wide.
R905.7	**Wood shingles**
R905.7.1	**Deck requirements.** Where spaced sheathing is used, sheathing boards shall not be less than 1-inch by 4-inch (25 mm by 102 mm) nominal dimensions and shall be spaced on centers equal to the weather exposure to coincide with the placement of fasteners.
R905.7.2	**Deck slope.** Wood shingles shall be installed on slopes of 3 units vertical in 12 units horizontal (25-percent slope) or greater.
Table R905.7.5(1)	**Wood Shingle Weather Exposure and Roof Slope**
R905.7.6	**Valley flashing.** Roof flashing shall not be less than No. 26 gage [0.019 inches (0.5 mm)]…Sections of flashing shall have an end lap of not less than 4 inches (102 mm).
R905.8	**Wood shakes**
R905.8.1	**Deck requirements.** Wood shakes shall be used only on solid or spaced sheathing.
R905.8.2	**Deck slope.** Wood shakes shall only be used on slopes of 3 units vertical in 12 units horizontal (25-percent slope) or greater.
Table R905.8.6	**Wood Shake Weather Exposure and Roof Slope**
R905.9	**Built-up roofs**
R905.9.1	**Slope.** Built-up roofs shall have a design slope of not less than 1/4 unit vertical in 12 units horizontal (2-percent slope) for drainage, except for coal-tar built-up roofs, which shall have a design slope of a minimum 1/8 unit vertical in 12 units horizontal (1-percent slope).
R905.9.2	**Material standards.** *Built-up roof covering* materials shall comply with the standards in Table R905.9.2 or UL 55A.

Section #	Highlight
R905.9.3	**Application.** Built-up roofs shall be installed in accordance with this chapter and the manufacturer's instructions.
R905.10	**Metal roof panels**
R905.10.1	**Deck requirements.** *Metal roof panel* roof coverings shall be applied to solid or spaced sheathing, except where the roof covering is specifically designed to be applied to spaced supports.
R905.10.2	**Slope.** Minimum slopes for metal roof panels shall comply with the following: (Highlight 1 – 3)
Table R905.9.2	**Built-Up Roofing Material Standards**
R905.11	**Modified bitumen roofing**
Table R905.11.2	**Modified Bitumen Roofing Material Standards**
R905.12	**Thermoset single-ply roofing**
R905.12.1	**Slope:** Thermoset *single-ply membrane* roofs shall have a design slope of a minimum of not less than ¼ unit vertical in 12 units horizontal (2-percent slope) for drainage.
R905.13	**Thermoplastic single-ply roofing**
R905.13.1	**Slope:** Thermoplastic *single-ply membrane* roofs shall have a design slope of not less than ¼ unit vertical in 12 units horizontal (2-percent slope).
R905.14	**Sprayed polyurethane foam roofing**
R905.14.1	**Slope.** Sprayed polyurethane foam roofs shall have a design slope of not less than ¼ unit vertical in 12 units horizontal (2-percent slope) for drainage.
R905.15	**Liquid-applied roofing**
R905.15.1	**Slope.** Liquid-applied roofing shall have a design slope of not less than ¼ unit vertical in 12 units horizontal (2-percent slope).
R906.1	**General.** Where above-deck thermal insulation is installed, such insulation shall be covered with an approved roof covering and shall comply with NFPA 276 or UL 1256.
Table R906.2	**Material Standards for Roof Insulation**
R1001.2	**Footings and foundations.** Footings for masonry fireplaces and their chimneys shall be constructed of concrete or *solid masonry* not less than 12 inches (305 mm) thick and shall extend not less than 6 inches (152 mm) beyond the face of the fireplace or foundation wall on all sides Footings shall be founded on natural, undisturbed earth or engineered fill below frost depth. In areas not subjected to freezing. footings shall be not less than 12 inches (305 mm) below finished *grade*.
R1001.5	**Firebox walls.** Masonry fireboxes shall be constructed of *solid masonry* units, *hollow masonry units* grouted solid, stone or concrete. Where a lining of firebrick not less than 2 inches (51 mm) thick or other *approved* lining is provided, the minimum thickness of back and sidewalls shall each be 8 inches (203 mm) of *solid masonry*, including the lining.
Table R1001.1	**Summary of Requirements for Masonry Fireplaces and Chimneys**

Section #	Highlight
R1001.7	**Lintel and throat.** Masonry over a fireplace opening shall be supported by a lintel of *noncombustible material*. The minimum required bearing length on each end of the fireplace opening shall be 4 inches (102 mm).
R1001.7.1	**Damper.** Masonry fireplaces shall be equipped with ferrous metal damper located not less than 8 inches (203 mm) above the top of the fireplace opening.
R1001.10	**Hearth extension dimensions.** Hearth extensions shall extend not less than 16 inches (406 mm) in front and not less than 8 inches (203 mm) beyond each side of the fireplace opening.
R1001.11	**Fireplace clearance.** Wood beams, joists, studs and other *combustible material* shall have a clearance of not less than 2 inches (51 mm) from the front faces and sides of masonry fireplaces and not less than 4 inches (102 mm) from the back faces of masonry fireplaces.
R1003.2	**Footings and foundations.** Footings for masonry chimneys shall be constructed of concrete or *solid masonry* not less than 12 inches (305 mm) thick and shall extend not less than 6 inches (152 mm) beyond the face of the foundation or support wall on all sides. Footings shall be founded on natural undisturbed earth or engineered fill below frost depth. In areas not subjected to freezing, footings shall be not less than 12 inches (305 mm) below finished *grade.*
R1003.5	**Corbeling.** Masonry chimneys shall not be corbelled more than one-half of the chimney's wall thickness from a wall or foundation, nor shall a chimney be corbeled from a wall or foundation that is less than 12 inches (305 mm) thick unless it projects equally on each side of the wall, except that on the second *story* of a two-story *dwelling*,
R1003.10	**Wall thickness.** *Masonry chimney* walls shall be constructed of *solid masonry* units or *hollow masonry units* grouted solid with not less than a 4-inch (102 mm) nominal thickness.
Table R1003.14(1)	**Net Cross-Sectional Area of Round Flue Sizes[a]**
Table R1003.14(2)	**Net Cross-Sectional Area of Square and Rectangular Flue Sizes**
R1003.17	**Masonry chimney cleanout openings.** Cleanout openings shall be provided within 6 inches (152 mm) of the base of the flue within every *masonry chimney*. The upper edge of the cleanout shall be located not less than 6 inches (152 mm) below the lowest chimney inlet opening. The height of the opening shall be not less than 6 inches (152 mm).
R1003.18	**Chimney clearances.** Any portion of a *masonry chimney* located in the interior of the building or within the exterior wall of the building shall have a minimum airspace clearance to combustibles of 2 inches (51 mm).
M1406.2	**Clearances.** Clearances for radiant heating panels or elements to any wiring, outlet boxes and junction boxes used for installing electrical devices or mounting luminaires shall comply with Chapters 34 through 43.
M1408.3	**Location:** 1. Floor registers of *floor furnaces* shall be installed not less than 6 inches (152 mm) from a wall. 6. The floor furnace shall not be installed in concrete floor construction built on grade.

Section #	Highlight

M1502.3   **Duct termination.** Exhaust ducts shall terminate on the outside of the building. Exhaust duct terminations shall be in accordance with the dryer manufacturer's installation instructions. If the manufacturer's instructions do not specify a termination location, the exhaust duct shall terminate not less than 3 feet (914 mm) in any direction from openings into buildings, including openings in ventilated soffits. Exhaust duct terminations shall be equipped with a backdraft damper.

M1502.4.3   **Transition duct.** Transition ducts used to connect the dryer to the exhaust *duct system* shall be a single length that is *listed* and *labeled* in accordance with UL 2158A. Transition ducts shall be not greater than 8 feet (2438 mm) in length.

M1502.4.6   **Duct length.** The maximum allowable duct length shall be determined by one of the methods in section M1502.4.6.1 or M1502.4.6.3.

M1803.3.1   **Floor, ceiling and wall penetrations.** A chimney connector or vent connector shall not pass through any floor or ceiling. A chimney connector or vent connector shall not pass through a wall or partition unless the connector is *listed* and *labeled* for wall pass-through, or is routed through a device *listed* and *labeled* for wall pass-through and is installed in accordance with the conditions of its *listing* and *label*.

Table M1803.3.4   **Chimney and Vent Connector Clearances to Combustible Materials**

M2005.2   **Prohibited locations.** Fuel-fired water heaters shall not be installed in a room used as a storage closet. Water heaters located in a bedroom or bathroom shall be installed in a sealed enclosure so that *combustion air* will not be taken from the living space.

G2403(202)   **General Definitions**

P2801.6   **Required pan.** Where a storage tank-type water heater or a hot water storage tank is installed in a location where water leakage from the tank will cause damage, the tank shall be installed in a pan constructed of one of the following: (Highlight 1 – 3)

P2801.6.1   **Pan size and drain.** The pan shall not be less than 1½ inches (38 mm) deep and shall be of sufficient size and shape to receive dripping or condensate from the tank or water heater.

P2801.6.2   **Pan drain termination.** The pan drain shall extend full-size and terminate over a suitably located indirect waste receptor or shall extend to the exterior of the building and terminate not less than 6 inches (152 mm) and not more than 24 inches (610 mm) above the adjacent ground surface.

P2804.3   **Pressure relief valves.** They shall be set to open not less than 25 psi (172 kPa) above the system pressure but not greater than 150 psi (1034 kPa).

P2804.4   **Temperature relief valves.** The valves shall be installed such that the temperature-sensing element monitors the water within the top 6 inches (152mm) of the tank.

P2902.3   **Backflow protection.** A means of protection against backflow shall be provided in accordance with sections P2902.3.1 through P2902.3.7.

International Residential Code 2018
Tabs and Highlights

These 1 Exam Prep Tabs are based on *International Residential Code, 2018 Edition*.

Each Tabs sheet has five rows of tabs. Start with the first tab at the first row at the top of the page, and proceed down that row placing the tabs at the locations listed below. Place each tab in your book setting it down one notch until you get to the bottom of the page, and then start back at the top again. After you have completed tabbing your book (the last tab is usually the glossary, appendix, or index), then you may start highlighting your book.

*****This concludes the tabs for this book. Please continue with the highlights on the following page.*****

A.M. 10/20/2021

Section #	Highlight

R101.2
Scope. shall apply to the construction, *alteration*, movement enlargement, replacement, repair, *equipment*, use and occupancy, location, removal and demolition of detached one- and two- family dwellings and *townhouses* not more than three stories above *grade plane* in height with a separate means of egress and their *accessory structures*.

R102.1
General. Where there is a conflict between a general requirement and a specific requirement, the specific requirement shall be applicable. Where, in any specific case, different sections of this code specify different materials, methods of construction or other requirements, the most restrictive shall govern.

R105.2
Work exempt from permit. *Permits* shall not be required for the following: **Building** 1 – 10.

R105.5
Expiration: Every *permit* issued shall become invalid unless the work is authorized by such *permit* is commenced within 180 days after its issuance.

R105.7
Placement of permit. The building *permit* or a copy shall be kept on the site of the work until completion of the project.

R106.3.1
Approval of construction documents. Where the *building official* issues a *permit*, the *construction documents* shall be *approved* in writing or by a stamp that states "REVIEWED FOR CODE COMPLIANCE."…*documents* so reviewed shall be retained by the *building official*. The other set shall be returned to the applicant, shall be kept at the site of work and shall be open to inspection by the *building official* or a duly authorized representative.

R107.1
General: Such *permits* shall be limited as to time of service, but not be permitted for more than 180 days.

R109.4
Approval required. Work shall not be done beyond the point indicated in each successive inspection without first obtaining the approval of the *building official*. The *building official*… to comply with this code. Any portions that do not comply shall be corrected and such portion shall not be covered or concealed until authorized by the *building official*.

R111.2
Temporary connection. The *building official* shall have the authority to authorize the temporary connection of the building or system to the utility, source of energy, fuel or power.

R114.1
Notice to owner or the owner's authorized agent. Upon notice from the *building official* that work on any building or structure is being executed contrary to the provisions of this code or in an unsafe and dangerous manner, such work shall be immediately stopped. The stop work order shall be in writing and shall be given to the owner of the property involved, or to the owner's authorized agent or to the person performing the work and shall state the conditions under which work will be permitted to resume.

R202
Definitions:
- [RB] BASEMENT
- [RB] BUILDING LINE
- [RB] DALLE GLASS
- [RB] DEAD LOADS
- [RB] DWELLING
- [RB] DWELLING UNIT
- [RB] LIVE LOADS
- [RB] PUBLIC WAY
- [RB] SKYLIGHT, UNIT
- [RB] SKYLIGHTS AND SLOPED GLAZING
- [RB] SUNROOM

Section #	Highlight
R301.1	**Application.** Building and structures, and all parts thereof, shall be constructed to safely… as prescribed by this code are deemed to comply with the requirements of this section.
R301.1.3	**Engineered design.** Where a building of otherwise conventional construction contains… code, these elements shall be designed in accordance with accepted engineering practice.
R301.2.1.2	**Protection of openings.** Glazed opening in windborne debris areas shall meet the requirements of the Large Missile Test of ASTM E1996 and ASTM as modified in Section 301.2.1.2.1.

Exception: Wood structural panels with a thickness of not less than 7/16 inch (11 mm) and a span of not more than 8 feet (2438 mm) shall be permitted for opening protection.

Attachment in accordance with Table R301.2.1.2 is permitted for buildings with a *mean roof height* of 45 feet (13728 mm) or less where the ultimate design wind speed, V_{ult}, is 180 mph (290 kph) or less. |
Table R301.2.1.2	**Windborne Debris Protection Fastening Schedule for Wood Structural Panels[a,b,c,d]**
R301.2.1.3	**Wind speed conversion.** the ultimate design wind speeds, V_{ult}, of Figure R301.2(5) shall be converted to nominal design wind speeds, V_{asd}, using Table R301.2.1.3.
Figure R301.2(4)	**Weathering Probability Map for Concrete[a,b]**
Figure R301.2(5)A	**Ultimate Design Wind Speeds**
Figure R301.2(7)	**Termite Infestation Probability Map**
Table R301.2.1.3	**Wind Speed Conversions[a]**
Table R301.6	**Minimum Roof Live Loads in Pounds-Force Per Square Foot of Horizontal Projection**
R310.1	**Emergency escape and rescue opening required.** Where *basements* contain…public way.
R310.2.1	**Minimum opening area.** Emergency escape and rescue openings shall have a net clear opening of not less than 5.7 square feet (0.530 m^2).
R310.2.2	**Window sill height.** Where a window is provided as the emergency escape and rescue opening, it shall have a sill height of not more than 44 inches (1118 mm) above the floor.
R310.2.3	**Window wells.** The horizontal area of the window well shall be not less than 9 square feet (0.9 m^2) with a horizontal projection and width of not less than 36 inches (914 mm).
R401.3	**Drainage.** Surface drainage shall be diverted to a storm sewer conveyance or other *approved* point of collection that does not create a hazard. *Lots* shall be graded to drain surface water away from foundation walls. The *grade* shall fall a minimum of 6 inches (152 mm) within the first 10 feet (3048 mm).
R401.4	**Soil tests.** Where quantifiable data created by accepted soil science methodologies indicate… This test shall be done by an *approved agency* using an *approved* method.
Table R401.4.1	**Presumptive Load-Bearing Values of Foundation Materials[a]**
R402.1	**Wood foundations.** Wood foundation systems shall be designed and installed in accordance with the provisions of this code.

38

Section #	Highlight
R402.1.1	**Fasteners:** Fasteners used below *grade* to attach plywood to the exterior side of exterior *basement* or crawl space wall studs, or fasteners used in knee wall construction shall be of... Electro-galvanized steel nails and galvanized (zinc coated) steel staples shall not be permitted.
R402.1.2	**Wood treatment.** Where lumber or plywood is cut or drilled after treatment, the treated... by repeated brushing, dipping or soaking until the wood cannot absorb more preservative.
R402.2	**Concrete.** Concrete shall have a minimum specified compressive strength of f'_c as shown in Table R402.2. Concrete subject...Materials used to produce concrete and testing thereof shall comply with the applicable standards listed in Chapters 19 and 20 of ACI 318 or ACI 332.
Table R402.2	**Minimum Specified Compressive Strength of Concrete**
R403.1.1	**Minimum size.** The minimum width, W, and thickness, T, for concrete footings shall be in accordance with Tables R403.1(1) through R403.1(3) and Figure R403.1(1) or R403.1.3.
	Footings for wood foundations shall be in accordance...Figures R403.1(2) and R403.1(3).
Table R403.1(1)	**Minimum Width and Thickness for Concrete Footings for Light-Frame Construction**
Figure R403.1(2)	**Permanent Wood Foundation Basement Wall Section**
Figure R403.1(3)	**Permanent Wood Foundation Crawl Space Section**
R403.1.4	**Minimum depth.** Exterior footings shall be placed not less than 12 inches (305 mm) below the undisturbed ground surface.
R403.1.7.3	**Foundation elevation.** On graded sites, the top of any exterior foundation shall extend above the elevation of the street that are at point of discharge or the inlet of an *approved* drainage device not less than 12 inches (305 mm) plus 2 percent.
R404.1.5	**Foundation wall thickness on walls supported**
R404.1.5.1	**Masonry wall thickness.** Masonry foundation walls shall not be less than the thickness of the wall supported, except that masonry foundation walls of not less than 8-inch (203 mm) nominal thickness shall be permitted under brick veneered frame walls and under 10-inch-wide (254 mm) cavity walls where the total height of the wall supported, including gables, is not more than 20 feet (6096 mm), provided that the requirements of Section R404.1.1 are met.
R404.1.6	**Height above finished grade.** Concrete and masonry foundation walls shall extend above the finished *grade* adjacent to the foundation at all points not less 4 inches (102 mm) were masonry veneer is used and a minimum of 6 inches (152 mm) elsewhere.
R404.1.8	**Rubble stone masonry.** shall have a minimum thickness 16 inches (406 mm), shall not support an unbalanced backfill exceeding 8 feet in height or soil pressure greater than 30 pounds per square foot per foot (4.71 kPa/m).
R404.3	**Wood sill plates.** shall be not less than 2-inch by 4-inch (51 mm by 102 mm) nominal lumber. Sill plate anchorage shall be in accordance with Sections R403.1.6 and R602.11.
R405.1	**Concrete or masonry foundations.** Drains shall be provided around concrete or masonry foundations that retain earth and enclose habitable or usable spaces located below *grade*.
	Gravel or crushed store drains shall extend at least 1 foot (305 mm) beyond the outside edge of the footing and 6 inches (152 mm) above the top of the footing and covered with an *approved* filter membrane material.

Section #	Highlight
	Drainage tiles or perforated pipe shall be placed on not less than 2 inches (51 mm) of washed gravel or crushed rock not less than one sieve size larger than the tile joint opening or perforation and covered with not less than 6 inches (152 mm) of the same material.
R406.2	**Concrete and masonry foundation waterproofing.** In areas where high water table or other severe soil water conditions are known to exist, exterior foundation walls that retain… Walls shall be waterproofed in accordance with one of the following: *Highlight* 1 – 8.
	Exception: Use of plastic roofing cements, acrylic coatings, latex coatings, mortars and pargings to seal ICF walls is permitted.
R407.3	**Structural requirements.** Wood columns shall not be less in nominal size than 4 inches by 4 inches (102 mm by 102 mm). Steel columns shall not be less than 3-inch-diameter (76 mm) Schedule 40 pipe manufactured in accordance with ASTM A 53 Grade B or *approved* equivalent.
R408.1	**Ventilation.** The minimum net area of ventilation openings shall be not less than 1 square foot (0.0929 m^2) for each 150 square feet (14 m^2) of under-floor space area, unless the ground surface is covered by a Class 1 vapor retarder material. Where a Class I vapor retarder material is used the minimum net area shall not be less than 1 sq. ft. for each 1,500 sq. ft.…One such ventilating opening shall be within 3 feet of each corner of the building.
R408.2	**Openings for under-floor ventilation.** Ventilation openings shall be covered for their height and width with any op the following materials provided that the least dimension of the covering shall not exceed 1/4 inch (6.4 mm): *Highlight* 1 – 6.
R408.4	**Access.** Access shall be provided for all under- floor spaces. Access openings through the floor shall be not smaller than 18 inches by 24 inches (457 mm by 610 mm). Openings… Through wall access openings shall not be located under a door to the residence.
R502.2.2	**Blocking and subflooring.** Blocking for fastening panel edges or fixtures shall be not less than utility grade lumber…in Section R503.2. Fireblocking shall be of any grade of lumber.
R502.11	**Wood trusses**
R502.11.1	**Design.** The truss design drawings shall be prepared…in accordance with Section R106.1.
R502.11.2	**Bracing.** Trusses shall be braced to prevent rotation…on individual truss design drawings.
R502.11.3	**Alterations to trusses.** *Alterations* resulting in the addition of load that exceeds the design load for the truss, shall not be permitted without verification that the truss is capable of supporting the additional loading.
R502.11.4	**Truss design drawings.** Truss design drawings shall include, at a minimum, the information specified below: *Highlight* 1 – 12.
R502.13	**Fireblocking required**
R503.1	**Lumber sheathing:** Maximum allowable spans for lumber used as floor sheathing shall conform to Tables R503.1, R503.2.1.1(1) and R503.2.1.1(2).
Table R503.1	**Minimum Thickness of Lumber Floor Sheathing**
R503.2	**Wood structural panel sheathing**
Table R503.2.1.1(2)	**Allowable Spans for Sanded Plywood Combination Subfloor Underlayment**[a]

Section #	Highlight
Table R503.2.1.1(1)	**Allowable Spans And Loads For Wood Structural Panels For Roof And Subfloor Sheathing And Combination Subfloor Underlayment[a,b,c]**
R503.2.2	**Allowable spans.** The maximum allowable span for wood structural panels used as subfloor or combination subfloor underlayment shall be set forth in Table R503.2.1.1(1), or APA E30.
R503.2.3	**Installation.** Wood structural panels used as subfloor or combination subfloor…R602.3(1) and shall be attached to cold-formed steel framing in accordance with Table R505.3.1(2).
R504.1.3	**Uplift and buckling.** Where required, resistance shall be provided to uplift or restraint against buckling shall be provided by interior bearing walls or properly designed stub walls anchored in the supporting soil below.
R504.2	**Site preparation.** The area within the foundation walls shall have all vegetation, topsoil and foreign material removed. The fill shall be compacted to ensure uniform support of the pressure preservative treated-wood floor sleepers.
R504.2.1	**Base.** A minimum 4-inch (102 mm) base granular base gravel maximum size ¾ inch (…) or crushed stone having a maximum size of ½ inch (…) shall be placed on compacted earth.
R504.2.2	**Moisture barrier.** Polyethylene sheeting of minimum 6-mil thickness shall be placed over the granular base. Joints shall be lapped 6 inches (152 mm) and left unsealed.
R506.1	**General.** Floors shall be a minimum 3½ inches (89 mm) thick (for expansive soils, see Section per R403.1.8).
R506.2	**Site preparation.** The area within the foundation walls shall have all vegetation, top soil and foreign material removed.
R506.2.1	**Fill.** Fill material shall be free of vegetation and foreign material. The fill shall be compacted …the fill depths shall not exceed 24 inches for clean sand or gravel and 8 inches for earth.
R506.2.2	**Base.** A 4-inch-thick (102 mm) base course consisting of clean grated sand, gravel, crushed stone, or blast furnace slag passing a 2-inch (51 mm) sieve shall be placed on the prepared subgrade when the slab is below *grade*. **Exception:** A base course is not required when the slab is installed on well-drained or sand-gravel mixture soils classified as Group I.
R506.2.3	**Vapor retarder.** A 6-mil polyethylene or *approved* vapor retarder with joints laps not less than 6 inches (152 mm) shall be placed between the concrete floor slab and the base course.
Table R602.3(1)	**Fastening Schedule**
R602.6	**Drilling and notching of studs.** 1. Notching 2. Drilling
R602.6.1	**Drilling and notching of top plate.** Where piping or ductwork is placed in or partly in an exterior wall or interior load-bearing wall, necessitating cutting, drilling or notching of the… at each side or equivalent. The metal tie must extend not less than 6 inches past the opening.
Figure R602.6(1)	**Notching And Bored Hole Limitations For Exterior Walls And Bearing Walls**
Figure R602.6(2)	**Notching And Bored Hole Limitations For Interior Nonbearing Walls**

Section #	Highlight
R702.5	**Other finishes.** Wood veneer paneling and hardboard paneling shall be placed on wood or cold-formed steel framing spaced not more than 16 inches (406 mm) on center…Wood veneer paneling not less than ¼-inch(6 mm) nominal thickness shall conform to ANSI/HPVA HP-1.
R703.2	**Water-resistive barrier.** One layer of No. 15 asphalt felt, free from holes and breaks, complying with ASTM D226 for Type 1 felt or other approved water-resistive barrier shall be applied over studs or sheathing of all exterior walls. No. 15 asphalt felt shall be applied… Where joints occur, felt shall be lapped not less than 6 inches (152 mm).
R703.5	**Wood, hardboard and wood structural panel siding**
R703.5.2	**Panel siding.** Vertical joints in panel siding shall occur over framing…Horizontal joints in panel siding shall be lapped not less than 1 inch (25 mm) or shall be shiplapped or flashed with Z-flashing and occur over solid blocking, wood or wood structural panel sheathing.
R703.6	**Wood shakes and shingles**
Table R703.6.1	**Maximum Weather Exposure for Wood Shakes and Shingles on Exterior Walls**[a,b,c]
R703.6.3	**Attachment.** Each shake or shingle shall be held in place by two stainless steel Type 304, Type 316 or hot-dipped zinc-coated…The fasteners shall penetrate the sheathing or furring strips by not less than ½ inch (13 mm) and shall not be overdriven.
R703.8	**Anchored Stone and masonry veneer, general**
R703.8.6	**Weepholes.** Weepholes shall be provided in the outside wythe of masonry walls at a maximum spacing of 33 inches (838 mm) on center. Weepholes shall be not less than 3/16 inch (5 mm) in diameter. Weepholes shall be located immediately above the flashing.
R703.10	**Fiber cement siding**
R703.10.1	**Panel siding.** Panels shall be installed with the long dimension either parallel or perpendicular to framing. Vertical and horizontal joints shall occur over framing members and shall be protected with caulking, or with battens or flashing, or be vertical or horizontal shiplap, or otherwise designed to comply with Section R703.1.
R703.10.2	**Lap siding.** Fiber-cement lap siding having a maximum width of 12 inches (305 mm) shall comply with ASTM C1186…Lap siding shall be lapped a minimum of 1¼ inches (32 mm) and lap siding not having tongue-and-groove should have the ends protected with caulking.
R802.1.5.4	**Labeling.** The label shall contain: *Highlight* 1 – 8.
R802.2	**Design and construction.** The roof and ceiling assembly shall provide continuous ties across the structure to prevent roof thrust from being applied to the supporting walls.
R802.4.2	**Framing details.** Rafters shall be framed not more than 1½ inches (38 mm) offset from each other to a ridge board or directly opposite from each other with a collar tie, gusset plate or ridge strap in accordance with Table R602.3(1).
Table R803.1	**Minimum Thickness of Lumber Roof Sheathing**
R806.1	**Ventilation required.** Ventilation openings shall have a least dimension of 1/16 inch (1.6 mm) minimum and ¼ inch (6.4 mm) maximum. Ventilation openings having a least dimension larger than ¼ inch (6.4 mm) shall be provided with corrosion-resistant wire cloth screening or similar with openings having a least dimension of 1/16 inch (1.6 mm) and ¼ inch (6.4 mm) maximum.

Section #	Highlight
R806.2	**Minimum vent area.** The minimum net free ventilating area shall be 1/150 of the area of the vented space.
R807.1	**Attic access.** Buildings with combustible ceiling or roof construction shall have an *attic* opening to *attic* areas that have a vertical height of 30 inches (762 mm) or greater over an area of not less than 30 square feet (2.8 m^2).
	The rough-framed opening shall not be less than 22 inches by 30 inches (559 mm by 762 mm) and shall be located in a hallway or other location with *ready access*.
R902.1	**Roofing covering materials.** Class A, B or C roofing shall be installed in jurisdictions designated by law as requiring their use or where the edge of the roof is less than 3 feet (914 mm) from a lot line.
R903.2	**Flashing.** Flashings shall be installed in a manner that prevents moisture from entering the wall and roof through joints in copings, through moisture permeable materials and at intersections with parapet walls and other penetrations through the roof plane.
R903.2.1	**Locations.** Flashings shall be installed at wall and roof intersections, wherever there is a change in roof slope or direction and around roof openings.
R903.3	**Coping.** Parapet walls shall be properly coped with noncombustible, weatherproof materials of a width no less than the cross section of the parapet wall.
R903.4	**Roof drainage.** Unless roofs are sloped to drain over roof edges, roof drains shall be installed at each low point of the roof.
R903.4.1	**Secondary (emergency overflow) drains and scuppers.** Overflow drains having the same size as the roof drains shall be installed with the…shall be installed in the adjacent parapet walls with the inlet flow located 2 inches (51 mm) above the low point of the roof served.
905.1.1	**Underlayment.** *Underlayment* materials required to comply with ASTM D226, D1970, D4869 and D6757 shall bear a label indicating compliance to the standard designation and, if applicable, type classification indicated in Table R905.1.1(1).
Table R905.1.1(1)	**Underlayment Types**
R905.2	**Asphalt shingles**
R905.2.2	**Slope.** Asphalt shingles shall be used only on roof slopes of two units in 12 units horizontal …double *underlayment* application is required in accordance with section R905.1.1.
R905.2.5	**Fasteners.** Fasteners for asphalt shingles shall be galvanized, stainless, aluminum or copper 12-gage [0.105 inch (3 mm)] shank with a minimum 3/8-inch-diameter (9.5 mm) head… materials and not less than ¾ inch (19.1 mm) into the roof sheathing. Where the roof sheathing is less than ¾ inch (19.1 mm) thick, the fasteners shall penetrate through the sheathing.
R905.2.6	**Attachment.** Asphalt shingles shall have the minimum number of fasteners required by the manufacturer's *approved* installation instructions, but not less than four fasteners per strip shingle or two fasteners per individual shingle. Where the roof slope exceeds 21 units vertical in 12 units horizontal (21:12, 175-percent slope), shingles shall be installed in accordance with the manufacturer's *approved* installation instructions.
R905.2.8.2	**Valleys.** Valley linings of the following types shall be permitted: *Highlight* 1 – 3.

44

Section #	Highlight
R905.2.8.5	**Drip edge.** Adjacent segments of drip edge shall be overlapped not less than 2 inches (51 mm) …deck not less than 2 inches (51 mm). Drip edges shall be mechanically fastened to the roof deck at not more than 12 inches (305 mm) o.c. with fasteners as specified in Section R905.2.5.
R905.3	**Clay and concrete tile**
R905.3.5	**Concrete tile.** Concrete roof tile shall comply with ASTM C1492.
R905.3.6	**Fasteners.** Nails shall be corrosion resistant and not less than 11-gage, 5/16-inch (11 mm) head, and of sufficient length to penetrate the deck not less than 3/4 inch (19 mm) or through the thickness of the deck, whichever is less.
R905.4	**Metal roof shingles**
R905.4.2	**Deck slope.** Metal roof shingles shall not be installed on roof slopes below three units vertical in 12 units horizontal (25-percent slope).
R905.4.6	**Flashing.** The valley flashing shall extend at least 8 inches (203 mm) from the centerline each way and shall have a splash diverter rib not less than 3/4 inch (19 mm) in height at…4 inches (102 mm). The metal valley flashing shall have a 36-inch-wide (914 mm) *underlayment*.
R905.6	**Slate shingles**
R905.6.3	**Underlayment.** *Underlayment* shall comply with Section R905.1.1.
Table R905.6.5	**Slate Shingle Headlap**
R905.6.6	**Flashing:** Valley flashing shall be not less than 15 inches (381 mm) wide.
R905.7	**Wood shingles**
R905.7.1	**Deck requirements.** Where spaced sheathing is used, sheathing boards shall not be less than 1-inch by 4-inch (25 mm by 102 mm) nominal dimensions and shall be spaced on centers equal to the weather exposure to coincide with the placement of fasteners.
R905.7.2	**Deck slope.** Wood shingles shall be installed on slopes of three units vertical in 12 units horizontal (25-percent slope) or greater.
Table R905.7.5(1)	**Wood Shingle Weather Exposure And Roof Slope**
R905.7.6	**Valley flashing.** Roof flashing shall not be less than No. 26 gage [0.019 inches (0.5 mm)]… and greater. Sections of flashing shall have an end lap of not less than 4 inches (102 mm).
R905.8	**Wood shakes**
R905.8.1	**Deck requirements.** Wood shakes shall be used only on solid or spaced sheathing.
R905.8.2	**Deck slope.** Wood shakes shall only be used on slopes of three units vertical in 12 units horizontal (25-percent slope) or greater.
Table R905.8.6	**Wood Shake Weather Exposure And Roof Slope**
R905.9	**Built-up roofs**
R905.9.1	**Slope.** Built-up roofs shall have a design slope of not less than one-fourth unit vertical in 12 units horizontal (2-percent slope) for drainage, except for coal-tar built-up roofs, which shall have a design slope of a minimum one-eighth unit vertical in 12 units horizontal (1-percent slope).

Section #	Highlight
R905.9.2	**Material standards.** shall comply with the standards in Table R905.9.2 or UL 55A.
R905.9.3	**Application.** Built-up roofs shall be installed in accordance with this chapter and the manufacturer's instructions.
R905.10	**Metal roof panels**
R905.10.1	**Deck requirements.** Metal roof panel roof panels shall be applied on solid or spaced sheathing except where the roof covering is specifically designed to be applied to spaced supports.
R905.10.2	**Slope.** Minimum slopes shall comply with the following: *Highlight* 1 – 3.
Table R905.9.2	**Built-Up Roofing Material Standards**
R905.11	**Modified bitumen roofing**
Table R905.11.2	**Modified Bitumen Roofing Material Standards**
R905.12	**Thermoset single-ply roofing**
R905.12.1	**Slope:** Thermoset single-ply roofs shall have a design slope of a minimum of not less than one-fourth unit vertical in 12 units horizontal (2-percent slope) for drainage.
R905.13	**Thermoplastic single-ply roofing**
R905.13.1	**Slope:** Thermoplastic single-ply roofs shall have a design slope of not less than one-fourth unit vertical in 12 units horizontal (2-percent slope).
R905.14	**Sprayed polyurethane foam roofing**
R905.14.1	**Slope.** Sprayed polyurethane foam roofs shall have a design slope of not less than one-fourth unit vertical in 12 units horizontal (2-percent slope) for drainage.
R905.15	**Liquid-applied roofing**
R905.15.1	**Slope.** Liquid-applied roofing shall have a design slope of not less than one-fourth unit vertical in 12 units horizontal (2-percent slope).
R906.1	**General.** The use of above-deck thermal insulation shall be permitted provided that such insulation is covered with an *approved* roof covering and complies with FM 4450 or UL 1256.
Table R906.2	**Material Standards for Roof Insulation**
R1001.2	**Footings and foundations.** Footings for masonry fireplaces and their chimneys shall be constructed of concrete or *solid masonry* at least 12 inches (305 mm) thick and shall extend at least 6 inches (152 mm) beyond the face of the fireplace or foundation wall on all sides… subjected to freezing. footings shall be not less than 12 inches (305 mm) below finished *grade*.
R1001.5	**Firebox walls.** Masonry fireboxes shall be constructed of *solid masonry* units, hollow masonry units grouted solid, stone or concrete. Where a lining of firebrick not less than 2 inches (51 mm) thick or other *approved* lining is provided, the minimum thickness of back and sidewalls shall each be 8 inches (203 mm) of *solid masonry*, including the lining.
Table R1001.1	**Summary of Requirements for Masonry Fireplaces and Chimneys**

Section #	Highlight
R1001.7	**Lintel and throat.** Masonry over a fireplace opening shall be supported by a lintel of noncombustible material. The minimum required bearing length on each end of the fireplace opening shall be 4 inches (102 mm).
R1001.7.1	**Damper.** Masonry fireplaces shall be equipped with ferrous metal damper located not less than 8 inches (203 mm) above the top of the fireplace opening.
R1001.10	**Hearth extension dimensions.** Hearth extensions shall extend not less than 16 inches (406 mm) in front and not less than 8 inches (203 mm) beyond each side of the fireplace opening.
R1001.11	**Fireplace clearance.** Wood beams, joists, studs and other combustible material shall have a clearance of not less than 2 inches (51 mm) from the front faces and sides of masonry fireplaces and not less than 4 inches (102 mm) from the back faces of masonry fireplaces.
R1003.2	**Footings and foundations.** Footings for masonry chimneys shall be constructed of concrete or *solid masonry* not less than 12 inches (305 mm) thick and shall extend not less than 6 inches (152 mm) beyond the face of the foundation or support wall on all sides.
	footings shall be not less than 12 inches (305 mm) below finished *grade*.
R1003.5	**Corbeling.** Masonry chimneys shall not be corbelled more than one-half of the chimney's wall thickness from a wall or foundation nor shall a chimney be corbeled from a wall or foundation that is less than 12 inches (305 mm) thick unless it projects equally on each side of the wall, except that on the second *story* of a two-story *dwelling*.
R1003.10	**Wall thickness.** Masonry chimney walls shall be constructed of *solid masonry* units or hollow masonry units grouted solid with not less than a 4-inch (102 mm) nominal thickness.
Table R1003.14(1)	**Net Cross Sectional Area of Round Flue Sizes[a]**
Table R1003.14(2)	**Net Cross Sectional Area of Square and Rectangular Flue Sizes**
R1003.17	**Masonry chimney cleanout openings.** Cleanout openings shall be provided within 6 inches of the base of the flue within every masonry chimney. The upper edge of the cleanout shall be located not less than 6 inches (152 mm) below the lowest chimney inlet opening. The height of the opening shall be not less than 6 inches (152 mm).
R1003.18	**Chimney clearances.** Any portion of a masonry chimney located in the interior of the building or within the exterior wall of the building shall have a minimum airspace clearance to combustibles of 2 inches (51 mm).
M1406.2	**Clearances.** Clearances for radiant heating panels or elements to any wiring, outlet boxes and junction boxes used for installing electrical devices or mounting luminaires shall comply with Chapters 34 through 43.
M1408.3	**Location:** 1. Floor registers of floor furnaces shall be installed not less than 6 inches from a wall. 6. The floor furnace shall not be installed in concrete floor construction built on grade.
M1502.3	**Duct termination.** Exhaust ducts shall terminate on the outside of the building. Exhaust duct terminations shall be in accordance with the dryer manufacturer's installation instructions. If the manufacturer's instructions do not specify a termination location, the exhaust duct shall terminate not less than 3 feet (914 mm) in any direction from openings into buildings. Exhaust duct terminations shall be equipped with a backdraft damper.

Section #	Highlight

M1502.4.3 **Transition duct.** Transition ducts used to connect the dryer to the exhaust *duct system* shall be a single length that is *listed* and *labeled* in accordance with UL 2158A. Transition ducts shall be not greater than 8 feet (2438 mm) in length.

M1502.4.5 **Duct length.** The maximum allowable duct length shall be determined by one of the methods in section M1502.4.5.1 or M1502.4.5.3.

M1803.3.1 **Floor, ceiling and wall penetrations.** A chimney connector or vent connector shall not pass through any floor or ceiling. A chimney connector or vent connector shall not pass through a wall or partition unless the connector is *listed* and *labeled* for wall pass-through, or is routed through a device *listed* and *labeled* for wall pass-through and is installed in accordance with the conditions of its *listing* and *label*.

Table M1803.3.4 **Chimney And Vent Connector Clearances to Combustible Materials[a]**

M2005.2 **Prohibited locations.** Fuel-fired water heaters shall not be installed in a room used as a storage closet. Water heaters located in a bedroom or bathroom shall be installed in a sealed enclosure so that *combustion air* will not be taken from the living space.

G2403(202) **General Definitions**

P2801.6 **Required pan.** Where a storage tank-type water heater or a hot water storage tank is installed in a location where water leakage from the tank will cause damage, the tank shall be installed in a pan constructed of one of the following: *Highlight* 1 – 3.

P2801.6.1 **Pan size and drain.** The pan shall not be less than 1½ inches (38 mm) deep and of sufficient size to receive all dripping or condensate from the tank or water heater.

P2801.6.2 **Pan drain termination.** The pan drain shall extend full-size and terminate over a suitably located indirect waste receptor or shall extend to the exterior of the building and terminate not less than 6 inches (152 mm) and not more than 24 inches (610 mm) above the adjacent ground surface.

P2804.3 **Pressure relief valves.** They shall be set to open not less than 25 psi (172 kPa) above the system pressure but not greater than 150 psi (1034 kPa).

P2804.4 **Temperature relief valves.** The valves shall be installed such that the temperature-sensing element monitors the water within the top 6 inches (152mm) of the tank.

P2902.3 **Backflow protection.** A means of protection against backflow shall be provided in accordance with sections P2902.3.1 through P2902.3.7.

Carpentry and Building Construction Manual, 2016 Ed.
Tabs and Highlights

These 1 Exam Prep Tabs are based on *Carpentry and Building Construction Book, 2016 Edition.*

Each Tabs sheet has five rows of tabs. Start with the first tab at the first row at the top of the page and proceed down that row placing the tabs at the locations listed below. Place each tab in your book setting it down one notch until you get to the bottom of the page, and then start back at the top again. After you have completed tabbing your book (the last tab is the glossary , appendix , or index), then you may start highlighting your book.

This concludes the tabs for this book. Please continue with the highlights on the following page.

35   **Permits and Inspections**

47   **Different Symbols** Highlight: Brick, Concrete Block, Cinder Block and Face Grain Wood.

49   **Using Plans:** The views of a building include general drawings and detail drawings… They provide information about how parts fit together.

50   **Plan Views:** A *site plan*, or *plot plan*, shows the building with lot boundaries…The basic elements of a site plan, are drawn from notes and sketches based upon a survey.

50 & 51   A *foundation plan* is a top view of the footings and foundation walls…This plan is used by foundation contractors.

55   **Detail Drawings:** When precise information is need about a small or complex portion of the building, a *detail drawing* is made.

           Details are drawn at larger scales than plan views, such as ½" = 1'0"…or ¼" = 1'0".

56   **Renderings:** A *rendering* is sometimes called a presentation drawing. It is more like a picture of the structure.

           Schedules: A **schedule** is a list or chart. (See example on page 57).

63   **Calculating Board Feet:** A **board foot** is a unit of measure that represents a piece of lumber… and the thickness of 1" nominal size.

           Table 2-3: Rules for Estimating Board Feet

           To determine the number of board feet in one or more pieces of lumber, use the following formula: (equation)

70   **Bar Charts:** A bar chart is an easy way to keep track of a project. It shows how long each tasks will take and when each task will start and end.

72   **Critical Path Method Diagrams:** The **Critical Path Method (CPM)** of scheduling shows the relationship among tasks as well as how long they take.

109 - 111   Highlight the following:

- Try Square
- Combination Square
- Sliding T-bevel
- Framing Square
- Triangular Framing Square
- Carpenter's Level
- Torpedo Level

218   **Understanding Concrete: Concrete** is a hard, strong building material that is made by mixing… water in proper proportions.

           Hydration is a chemical reaction that occurs when water combines with cement.

219   **Table 8-1: Basic Types of Portland Cement**

Page#	**Highlight**
	Mixing and Placing Mortar: Mortar stiffened by hydration should be thrown away. It is not easy to tell whether evaporation or hydration is the cause.
	Building the Corners: The corners of the wall are built first, usually four or five courses high.
281	A **story pole**, or course pole, is a board with markings 8" apart. It can be used to gauge the top of the masonry for each course.
285	**Table: Estimating Table for Masonry Blocks**
287	**Lintels and Bond Beams:** Where openings occur in the foundation, a *lintel* must be installed over the opening to provide support for the masonry above it. A lintel…One leg of the L fits under the masonry to support it over the opening. Another type of lintel is made of…It is placed over an opening just as a wood header would be placed. A third way to create a lintel is to use lintel…The open portions of the blocks are then filled with concrete and reinforced with rebar.
	A bond beam is a course of reinforced concrete or reinforced lintel block. It is sometimes called a *collar beam.*
294	**Fountain Slab Basics: Concrete flatwork** consist of flat, horizontal areas of concrete that are usually 5" or less in thickness.
303	**Table 11-1: Estimating Materials for Concrete Slab**
304	**Screeding:** The first step in finishing any flatwork is screeding…Screeding may also be done with mechanical equipment.
305	**Bullfloating:** Bullfloating makes the concrete surface more even with no high or low spots.
	Bullfloating is done shortly after screeding, while the concrete is still wet enough…there must be no visible water on the concrete.
	Edging and Jointing: When the sheen has left the surface and the concrete has started to stiffen, other finishing operations can be done…The edger is run back and forth, covering coarse aggregate particles.
306	**Troweling:** For a dense, smooth finish, floating is followed by troweling with a steel trowel … Troweling cannot be started until the concrete has hardened enough to prevent fine material and water from working to the surface.
320	**Hardwoods and Softwoods**
	Table 12-1: Principal Commercial Softwoods
324	**Hardwood Grades:** Hardwood are available in three common grades, *first and seconds* (FAS), *select*, and *No. 1 common.*
	Figure: A Grade Stamp. Know each mark (A) – (E).
353	**Engineered Lumber Basics:** Engineered lumber is not suitable for all purposes. It should not be used where it will permanently be exposed to the weather.
382	**Table 14-2: Floor Joist Spans**
403	**Table 15-2: Floor Joist Spans for Common Lumber Species**

605   **Garage Doors:** Mounting clearance required above the top of sectional overhead doors is usually about 12". However, low headroom brackets are available when such clearance is not possible. Overhead doors are usually installed by the door supplier.

608   **Preparing the Door:** When hung properly, the door should fit with an opening clearance of 1/16" at the sides and top…If it has a threshold, the bottom clearance should be 1/8" above the threshold.

Bevel the lock edge so that the inside edge will clear the jamb. This angle is about 3°.

615   **Interior Doors:** Most interior passage doors are 1-3/8" thick. Standard interior door height is 6'-8'. Common minimum widths for single doors are as follows:

-Bedrooms and other habitable rooms: 2'-6"

-Bathrooms: 2'- 4"

-Small closets and linen closets: 2'

617   **Pocket Doors:** A *pocket door* slides into an opening or pocket inside a wall.

Standard widths are 2'-0", 2'-4", 2'-6", 2'-8", and 3'-0". Any style of door with a thickness of 1-3/8" can be installed in the pocket to match the other doors in the home.

618   **Installing Interior Doors**

619   **Installing the Door Frame:** Plumb the assembled frame in the rough opening using pairs of shingle shims placed between the side jambs and the studs.

Hanging an Interior Door: Interior doors are often hung with two 3½" by 3½" loose-pin butt hinges. However, three hinges will strengthen the door and help to prevent it from warping.

620   **Door Stops and Trim:** After the door is in place, permanently nail the stops with 1½" finish nails. Nail the stop on the lock side first, setting it tightly against the door face while the door is latched. Space the nails 16" apart in pairs…Allow a 1/32" clearance from the door face to prevent scraping as the door is opened.

626   **Roofing Terms & Concepts:** One **square** of roofing is the amount of roofing required to cover 100 sq. ft. of roof surface. The amount of weather protection provided by the overlapping of shingles is called *coverage*.

629   **Roll Roofing**

632   **Underlayment:** *Underlayment* is a layer of weather-resistant material that is applied to the roof sheathing before the final roofing material is installed.

Roof underlayment generally has four purposes: (4 Bullets)

633   Eaves protection should extend from the end of the eaves to a point at least 22" inside the exterior wall line of the house.

Flashing: Flashing is a thin metal sheet or strip used to protect a building from water seepage.

Flashing must be installed so that it sheds water. Metal used for flashing must be corrosion resistant. Galvanized steel (at least 26 gauge), 0.019" thick aluminum, 16 oz. copper, or lead-coated copper can be used.

Page#	Highlight

634 **Drip Edges:** *Drip edges* are designed and installed to protect edges of the roof.

636 **Installing Underlayment:** Make sure to create a top lap of at least 2" at all horizontal joints and a 4" side lap at all end joints. Lap the underlayment over all hips and ridges for 6" on each side.

637 **Laying Shingles**

638 Two methods for alignment are:

- *Method 1:* Breaking the joints on halves

- *Method 2:* Breaking the joints on thirds

Nailing: Nails should be made of hot-dipped galvanized steel, aluminum, or stainless steel … Shanks should be 10-to 12-gauge wire.

In areas where high, local codes may require six nails per shingle…To provide extra resistance to uplift in high wind areas, use six nails for each strip.

642 **Table 22-1: Determining Roof Area from a Plan**

652 **Installation:** To ensure the correct slope, measure the distance in feet from one end of the fascia to the other. Round up to the nearest whole foot. Multiply this number by 1/16".

658 **Types of Wood Siding**

660 **Flashing:** Metal flashing is used to seal the joints where the siding meets a horizontal surface… Flashing should extend well under the siding and sufficiently over ends of a well-sloped drip cap to prevent water from seeping in.

661 **Protecting the Sheathing:** sheathing should be covered by a barrier or building paper or housewrap…Every type of siding should be installed over building paper or housewrap.

663 **Sizes:** The top edge is 3/16" thick in all sizes.

690 **Brick Basics**

694 **Types of Mortar**

- Type M
- Type S
- Type N
- Type O

697 **Figure: Brick Veneer at The Foundation**

698 **Flashing and Drainage:** A **weep hole** is a hole that provides drainage near the bottoms of the walls. Weep holes are often formed…every 18" to 24" along the wall.

Wall Ties: The veneer wall must be tied to the frame of the house with corrosion-resistant fasteners, called *wall ties*, secured with galvanized nails.

1 Exam Prep
Carpentry and Building Construction Manual, 2010 Edition
Tabs and Highlights

These 1 Exam Prep Tabs are based on the *Carpentry and Building Construction Book, 2010 Edition.*

Each 1 Exam Prep Tabs sheet has five rows of tabs. Start with the first tab at the first row at the top of the page; proceed down that row placing the tabs at the locations listed below. Place each tab in your book setting it down one notch until you get to the bottom of a page. Then start back at the top again.

1 Exam Prep Tab	Page #	Highlight
Table of Contents	v	Table of Contents
Building Codes & Planning	35	Permits and Inspections
	47	Figure 2-12: Different Symbols Highlight: Brick, Concrete Block, Cinder Block and Face Grain Wood
Plans & Drawings	49	The views of a building include general drawings and detail drawings … They provide information about how parts fit together.
	50	Plan Views: Definition of site plan. "The basic elements of a site plan, such as the one shown in Figure 2-14, are drawn from notes and sketches based upon a survey. …This plan is used by foundation contractors."
	55	Detail Drawings: Definition of detail drawing. See example in Figure 2-19.
	56	Rendering: Definition of rendering. See example in Figure 2-20. Definition of schedule.
	57	See example in Figure 2-21.
Calculating Board Feet	63	Calculating Board Feet: Definition of board foot. See Figure 2-26. Rules for estimating board feet. See Table 2-3. Formula to determine the number of board feet in lumber.
Bar Chart	70	Bar Charts: Definition of bar chart. See example in Figure 2-28.

Wall Form Details: "Wall forms may be made from wood or metal, depending on how durable they must be. Many are made from plywood and lumber. Although any exterior-grade plywood can be used, special form-grade plywood is available."

Definition of plyform

Definition of medium-density overlay (MDO)

Definition of high-density overlay (HDO)

Definition of mill-oiled plywood

"Forms built on site may be taken apart after the concrete hardens. The lumber can then be reused elsewhere in the project. It is generally more cost effective and efficient to use reusable forms."

Sill-Plate Anchors

Definition of sill sealer. See example in Figure 10-12.

Foundation Wall Details

Strengthening Walls: Definition of pilaster

Protecting Block Walls: "Care must be taken to keep blocks dry on the job. They should be stored on planks or other supports so the edges do not touch the ground. They should be covered for protection against moisture. Concrete block must not get wet just before or during installation."

Mortar Mixtures

Definition of Type N mortar

Definition of Type M mortar

Definition of Type S mortar

Definition of Type O mortar

Table 10-4: Proportions of Mortar Ingredients by Volume

Mixing and Placing Mortar: "Mortar stiffened by hydration should be thrown away. It is not easy to tell whether evaporation or hydration is the cause."

	Page #	Highlight
Door & Window Details	759	Door Casing
	760-761	Window Casing and Shutters: Definition of stool
		Definition of apron
		See example of stool and apron in Figure 26-14
		"The window stool is normally the first piece of window trim to be installed. It is notched so that it fits between the jambs and butts against the lower sash. Refer to Figure 26-15. The upper drawing shows the stool in place. The lower drawing shows it laid out and cut, ready for installation."
Cabinets & Countertops	780-781	Planning for Cabinets
	783-784	"Wall cabinets are usually 12" deep and are often located beneath a soffit.
		Definition of soffit.
Insulation/R-Value	894-895	Definition of R-value
		Table 31-1: Thermal Properties of various Building Material per Inch of Thickness
	900	Controlling Moisture: Definition of condensation and example.
	901	Attic Ventilation
	902	"Where a sloped ceiling is insulated, there should be a free opening of at least 1-1/2" between the sheathing and the insulation to encourage are movement."
	906	See "Job Safety" Box: Handling Fiberglass
Suspended Ceiling	938-939	Installing a Suspended Ceiling (Steps 1-7)
	941	Acoustical Ceilings: Definition of Acoustical Ceiling
Finish Flooring	972-973	Wood Flooring Basics
	975	Storage and Handling of Wood Flooring: "Never unload wood flooring when it is raining or snowing...Never store wood flooring directly in contact with a concrete floor."
Laying Tongue & Groove	979	Laying Strip Flooring

The Contractor's Guide to Quality Concrete Construction, 4th Ed

.

Tabs and Highlights

These 1 Exam Prep Tabs are based on *The Contractor's Guide to Quality Concrete Construction, 4th Edition*.

Each Tabs sheet has five rows of tabs. Start with the first tab at the first row at the top of the page, and proceed down that row placing the tabs at the locations listed below. Place each tab in your book setting it down one notch until you get to the bottom of the page, and then start back at the top again. After you have completed tabbing your book (the last tab is the glossary, appendix, or index), then you may start highlighting your book.

This concludes the tabs for this book. Please continue with the highlights on the following page.

A.M. 08/10/2021

Page	Highlight

Page   **Highlight**

11   ***Slump (ASTM C143/C143M):*** The slump test is used to measure the consistency of the concrete …Variations in slump are caused by changes in water content, air content, admixtures, aggregate proportions and gradation, concrete age, and temperature.

12   ***Fig. 2.2–Measuring the slump of fresh concrete. The cone is filled with concrete in three layers of equal volume (Steps 1, 2, and 3). Each layer is rodded 25…with a steel tamping rod.***

Compressive strength tests (ASTM C31/31M and C39/C39M): The compressive strength of concrete is measured by testing concrete cylinders–either 6 in. in diameter and 12…Cylinders are tested for two purposes: for acceptance testing (to determine whether the concrete delivered to the job meets the specified strength) and to estimate the strength of the concrete at a given time.

14   ***Fig. 2.5a–Cylinders must be kept at a controlled temperature while stored on the jobsite.***

14 & 15   ***Basic types of portland cement:***

1. Type I: general-purpose
2. Type II: reduced heat of hydration / moderate sulfate resistance
3. Type III: high-early-strength
4. Type IV: low heat-of-hydration / lowest early strength
5. Type V: sulfate-resistant / lower early strength

15   ***Fly ash:*** Fly ash is a byproduct of coal-burning power plants and is classified as a pozzolan.

16   Fly ash usually reduces the air content in air-entrained concrete, so a larger amount of air-entraining agent is needed to maintain the required amount of air.

19   **Admixtures:** Admixtures, when properly used, can increase early strength, increase ultimate strength, accelerate…They are dispensed into the batch in measured amount in a liquid form.

Water reducers: Water-reducing admixtures enhance the workability of the concrete, making it possible to reduce the water by 5 percent or more.

High-range water-reducing admixtures: Commonly known as superplasticizers, high-range water-reducing (HRQR) admixtures may reduce the amount of water in the mix by over 30 percent (Fig. 2.11) while keeping the slump constant.

Retarders: A retarder is usually used in hot weather to extend setting time, allowing more time for placement and finishing, and often causing a reduction in early strength.

Accelerators: An accelerator is used to shorten setting time or to produce high early strengths.

20   ***Air-entraining agents:*** In addition to being essential for durability, entrained air benefits concrete in other ways.

22   **Table 2.3 Relationship between water-cement ratio and compressive strength of concrete**

24   **Table 2.5 Maximum permissible water-cementitious ratios for concrete in severe exposures**

38   **Delivery Time for Ready Mixed Concrete:** Unless special conditions are involved, the maximum delivery time (…) is specified as 90 minutes.

74   **Placing Concrete in Forms:** Freshly mixed concrete must be properly consolidated after it is… form vibrators requires special form design to determine the power output and location of the vibrators because external vibration can destroy a form that is not designed for such loading.

Fig. 5.25–An internal vibrator causes the concrete within its field of action to act like a thick liquid and thus consolidate better.

91	**Types of Reinforcement:** Though most reinforcement for concrete is made of steel, today's concrete reinforcement can also be manufactured from (FRP) and other synthetic materials.

The most commonly used types of reinforcement are deformed bars and WWR.

94	Deformed bars are round steel bars with deformations (sometimes called lugs or protrusions) rolled into the surface of the bar.

Table 6.1 ASTM Standard metric reinforcing bars

95	*Welded wire reinforcement*

Other types of reinforced concrete: (*FRC*) Fibered-reinforced concrete has dispersed, randomly oriented fibers added to the concrete mixture.

99	**Storing and Handling Reinforcing Bars On The Job:** Before reinforcing bars are placed, many inspectors require that the bar surface be free of any coatings that might reduce the bond between concrete and steel.

A thin film of rust or mill scale is normal and is not harmful, but loose rust or mill scale should be brushed off.

100	**Concrete Cover**

Fig. 6.16–Minimum cover requirements.

Table 6.3 Minimum cover for cast-in-place concrete per ACI 318

102	**Placing of Reinforcement:** Reinforcing bars must be held securely in position while the concrete is being placed. This is accomplished by tying the bars together at certain intersections with tie wire, usually No. 16 gage (1.31 mm^2) black, soft annealed wire.

There are different types of rebar ties:

- Type A, called a single tie, are the simplest and are normally used in flat horizontal work.
- Type B, called a wrap-and-snap tie, are for tying wall reinforcement.
- Type C, saddle or U-ties, are more complicated and are used for tying footing bars or mats to hold hooked ends in bars in position; they are used also to secure column ties to vertical bars.
- Type D, called a wrap-and-saddle ties, are similar to the saddle tie and can be used to secure heavy mats that are lifted by cranes.
- Type E, figure-eight ties, can be used in walls instead of the wrap-and-snap tie.
- Epoxy-coated tie wire is typically required to tie epoxy-coated reinforcing steel.

103	*Fig. 6.21–The most common ties.*
104	**Bar Supports and Spacers:** Wire bar supports are classified into three classes for rust protection

- *Class 1 (maximum protection)*
- *Class 1A (maximum protection)*
- *Class 2 (moderate protection)*
- *Class 3 (no protection)*

<u>Page</u>	<u>Highlight</u>

1 Exam Prep

The Contractors Guide to Quality Concrete Construction , 3rd Edition

Tabs and Highlights

These 1 Exam Prep Tabs are based on The Contractor's Guide to Quality Concrete Construction, 3rd Edition.

Each 1 Exam Prep Tabs sheet has five rows of tabs. Start with the first tab at the first row at the top of the page; proceed down that row placing the tabs at the locations listed below. Place each tab in your book setting it down one notch until you get to the bottom of a page. Then start back at the top again.

Special Note to our Students: If you are a 1 Exam Prep student, here is how to really get the most from these Tabs. Follow the above instructions , but before placing the tab, find the tab's topic in the outline of your appropriate module. Now locate and highlight several items listed in the outline just before the topic, and just after. See how the topic fits in the outline and how it relates as a concept to the broader concept spelled out in the outline. If you take a few minutes to do this, when you take the test key words in the test questions will remind you of where the information is in the manual!

54   **Placing Concrete in the Forms:** Freshly mixed concrete must be properly consolidated after it is deposited into the form if it is to achieve its desired material properties…..The use of external form vibrators requires special form design to determine the power output and location of the vibrators because external vibration can destroy a form that is not designed for such loading.

54   **Figure 5.22** - An internal vibrator causes the concrete within its field of action to act like a thick liquid and thus consolidate better…

Reinforcement   63   CHAPTER 6

66   **Types of Reinforcement**: Though most reinforcement for concrete is made of steel, today's concrete reinforcement can also be manufactured from plastic and other synthetic materials…..

66   The most commonly used types of reinforcement are deformed bars and welded wire reinforcement.

66   Deformed bars are round steel bars with lugs rolled into the surface of the bar. There are 11 ASTM standard bar sizes (See Table 6.1).

68   Another type of reinforcement is welded wire fabric…..Welded wire reinforcement is commonly (but incorrectly) called mesh". WWR is shipped in rolls or flat sheets

68   **Other Types of Reinforced Concrete:** Fibered-reinforced concrete has dispersed, randomly oriented fibers added to the concrete mix.

72   **Storing and Handling Reinforcing Bars on the Job**: Before reinforcing bars are placed, many inspectors require that the bar surface be free of any coatings that might reduce the bond between concrete and steel.

72   A thin film of rust or mill scale is normal and is not harmful, but loose rust or mill scale should be brushed off.

72   Concrete cover: Example: Number 5 and smaller 1 ½ inches. (Also See Fig. 6.12)

74   **Placing of Reinforcement:** Reinforcing bars must be held securely in position while the concrete is being placed… usually No. 16 gage black, soft annealed wire

74-75   There are many different types of rebar ties:
          - Type A: Called a single tie, are the simplest and are normally used in flat horizontal work
          - Type B: Called a wrap-and-snap tie, are for tying wall reinforcement
          - Type C: Saddle or "U" ties, are more complicated and are used for tying footing bars or mats to hold hooked ends in bars in position; they are used also to secure column ties to vertical bars
          - Type D: Called a wrap-and-saddle ties, are similar to the saddle tie and can be used to secure heavy mats that are lifted by cranes

75   - Type E: Figure eight ties, can be used in walls instead of the wrap-and-snap tie

75   **Figure 6.14** -The most common ties.

76   **Splicing Reinforcing Steel**: The three types of splices are:
- Lap Splices: May be more economical than the other types of splices, depending on the amount of congestion and labor productivity. In lap splices, the bars are lapped next to each other a certain length and securely wired together with tie wire.
- Mechanical Splices: Use two basic splicing devices: couplers and end-bearing. Couplers are used to resist both tensile and compressive forces. End-bearing devices are used for splices capable of transferring compression forces only.
- Welded Splices: Are generally lap splices or butt splices, of which there are several types. Another process, called thermite welding, is used in making butt-welded joints in large size bars, particularly #43 and #57 bars.

Joints and Embedments   79   CHAPTER 7

79   Three types of joints are used in concrete slabs and walls:
- Contraction Joints: Are made within a structural element or building to accommodate movements that are caused by temperature changes, drying, shrinkage, and creep…
-Isolation Joints: Are used at points of restraint, including the junction between the elements of a structure…..
- Construction Joints: Are joints that are introduced for the convenience or needs of the construction process…

79   Be familiar with: **Construction Joints for Supported Beams & Slabs**

80   Be familiar with: **Contraction Joints for Walls**

81   **Isolation Joints for Walls**

82   **Construction Joints in Walls**
- Horizontal Construction Joints
- Vertical Construction Joints

Joints and Reinforcement   87   CHAPTER 8

88   **Contraction (Control) Joints:** Contraction joints are not intended to prevent cracks…..These planned cracks at the contraction joints are usually induced by cutting into the slab to a depth of one-fourth the slab thickness, or a minimum of 1 in. creating a weakened plane.

90   **Contraction Joint Spacing:** A common guideline for spacing contraction joints is to space them in feet approximately 2-½ times the slab depth in inches… under less than average conditions as little as two times the depth of the slab.

91   Isolation Joints (Expansion Joints): Isolation joints are used to separate the slab from any adjacent structure such as another slab, wall, column, adjacent building, or any appurtenance in the slab.
- Junction of slab and wall
- Columns

92   **Reinforcement in a Concrete Slab**: Reinforcement in a slab includes reinforcing bars, welded wire fabric, steel and synthetic fibers, smooth dowels, and tie bars.….Tie bars are used to prevent adjacent slabs from separating at warping joints or to tie the outside or perimeter lane in a large paved area to the adjacent lane

92   **Welded Wire Reinforcement**: To serve its purpose, the WWR should be placed 2 in. below the slab surface or within the upper one-third of the slab thickness, whichever is closer to the surface.….Hooks may be used to pull up low spots after screeding but before initial floating.

124   **Pumping Concrete:** Because the concrete pumping must be continuous, trucks scheduling is extremely important. A long delay may require having to break down the line, clean it out, and start again

125   **Finishing a Slab-on-Ground:** A checkrod follows screeding to fill in minor low spots or cut off high points and to embed coarse aggregate particles into the surface.

126   **Surface Finishes:** Properly done, a troweled surface will be hard, dense, and extremely wear-resistant.….This procedure avoids the problems caused by over-troweling or troweling overly-wet surfaces

126   **Figure 10.16** - Timely power floating…

        Figure 10.18 - Hand troweling for the final finish…

        Figure 10.19 - Applying a broomed finish for a uniform and skid-resistant surface

127   **Controlling Placement**: In wall and column placement, the distance of free fall of the concrete may have to be controlled. High slump, non-air-entrained mixes are most likely to segregate, possibly at heights of more than 5 or 6 ft. When segregation may be a problem, dropchutes (elephant trunks) may be used (Fig 10.21). Splashing can also be eliminated by use of dropchutes

Modern Masonry, Ninth Edition
Tabs and Highlights

These 1 Exam Prep Tabs and Highlights are based on *Modern Masonry: Brick, Block, Stone, Ninth Edition*.

Each Tabs sheet has five rows of tabs. Start with the first tab at the first row at the top of the page and proceed down that row placing the tabs at the locations listed below. Place each tab in your book setting it down one notch until you get to the bottom of the page, and then start back at the top again. After you have completed tabbing your book (the last tab is usually the glossary, appendix, or index), then you may start highlighting your book.

Running bond

Common bond or *American bond*

Flemish bond (half bricks are called clipped or *snap headers*)

Garden wall bond

Double stretcher garden wall bond

English bond

English cross or *Dutch bond*

Block or *stack bond*

7.8.4 Mortar Joints: Mortar joints use mortar between brick units to perform one or more of the following functions. (4 Bullets)

Concave joints

V-shaped joints: Because these two joints are compacted, they effectively prevent rain from penetrating into the joint. Their use is recommended where heavy rains and high winds are likely to occur. The concave joint is the most popular mortar joint.

Unglazed Facing Tile: This type is also best where the following characteristics are important:

- A high degree of mechanical perfection

Sizes and Shapes: Sizes are usually given in their nominal dimensions. A unit measuring 7 5/8' wide, 7 5/8' high, and 15 5/8" long is known as an 8" x 8" x 16" unit. The mortar joint is intended to be 3/8" to fit the modular design based on a 4" module.

The two-core design has the following advantages: (4 Bullets)

8.2.5 Glass Block: Glass blocks are manufactured in three popular sizes – 5 ¾ inches square, 7 ¾ inches square, and 11 ¾ inches square. See **Figure 8-37**. All of these sizes are 3 7/8" thick. A ¼" mortar joint is required.

Figure 8-37. Glass Block Layout Table

9.5 Stone Applications: Limestone is an excellent sill material that can be used on exterior masonry walls. See **Figure 9-14**. The fact that it is one piece ensures better protection against water leakage.

10.1 Mortar Materials: Mortar is general made up of cementitious (cement-like) materials together with sand and water.

10.1.1 Cementitious Materials: Cementitious materials include Portland cement (Type I, II, or III), masonry cements, and hydrated lime (Type S).

Hydrated Lime: Hydrated lime is quicklime that has been slacked before packaging. *Slacked* means the quicklime has been formed into putty by combining it with water.

10.3.4 Retempering Mortar: Workability can be restored by adding the lost water and mixing briefly (*retempering*).

Mortar should be used and placed in final position within 2 1/2 hours after mixing to avoid hardening due to hydration.

191   **10.4.2 Properties of Hardened Mortar:** The compressive strength of mortar increases as the cement content is increased and decreases as lime is increased.

Bond strength is the most significant property of hardened mortar, but it is also the most difficult to predict.

10.5.1 Type M Mortar: It is useful for unreinforced masonry below grade and in contact with earth. Such structures include foundations, retaining walls, walks, sewers and manholes.

191 & 192   **10.5.2 Type S Mortar:** Type S is recommended for the following applications: (Bullet #2 Only)

- Unreinforced masonry where maximum flexural (bending) strength is required

197   **Figure 10-10. Mortar Needed for Concrete Masonry Units**

205   **11.1.1 Types of Ties**

Unit Ties: Three types of unit ties are used in masonry wall construction. They are rectangular ties, Z ties, and corrugated ties.

209   **Figure 11-11.** Adjustable assemblies in typical applications.

213   **Figure 11-22.** A strap anchor being put into place connecting a partition wall into a bearing wall.

223   **Cutting Brick with a Brick Hammer:** This procedure produces a rough cut, but is acceptable for applications where the cut edge is hidden by mortar.

229   **12.2.4 Using a Corner Pole and Gauge Stick:** A *corner pole*, sometimes referred to as a *story pole*, is a narrow board that is generally 1" x 2" and 8' – 10' long (about one story in height). A corner pole is used to measure the mortar joint heights of each course of masonry.

245   **Tie Placement/Joint Reinforcement:** The most important factors affecting performance of wall ties are as follows: (Bullet #3 Only)

- Full bedding of the bed joint and placing the wall tie in the mortar 5/8" from either edge of the masonry unit.

252   **12.5.1 Cleaning Brick:** A solution of hydrochloric acid is used extensively as a cleaning agent for new masonry.

254   **Abrasive Blasting:** For best results, use a very low pressure (60-100 psf) and softer materials that will not damage the exterior surface of the brick.

260   **13.2.3 Cavity Walls:** A *cavity wall is a two-wythe* wall that allows each wythe to react independently to stress. Cavity walls usually consist of two walls separated by a continuous air space that is at least 2" wide. The 2" cavity is the most common.

262   **13.2.5 Veneered Walls:** Metal ties are used in residential veneer construction to anchor the veneer to the frame or masonry backing.

266   **13.3.2 Handling Concrete Blocks:** Position blocks in a wall with the wide flange on the top to provide a wider space for the bed joint.

Page#	Highlight
268	**13.3.5 Using a Mason's Line:** The twig is a thin piece of metal designed to hold the line between its metal fingers. Twigs may also be made of plastic with the line snapped into the twig. The single block is set at the correct height using the proper amount of mortar to ensure that the final top edge of the block is at the same elevation as its corner leads. Stay a line width (1/16") away from the line so you do not risk moving the line, which would destroy its usefulness as a reference guide.
272	**13.4.1 Laying an 8" Running Bond Concrete Block Wall - Procedure:** 11. A 5/8" diameter bar is usually used for a 3/8" concave mortar joint.
274	**13.4.2 Control Joints in a Concrete Block Wall:** They should be sealed with caulking compound after the mortar has been raked out to a depth of 3/4".
316	**15.3.1 Dampproofing and Waterproofing Basement Walls:** Cover the wall from the footing to 6" above the finished grade line.
328	**16.1.2 Four-Inch RBM Curtain and Panel Walls:** Curtain walls can be anchored to columns, spandrel beams, floors, or bearing walls, but are not necessarily built between structural elements. These walls must support their own weight for the height of the wall.
336	**Lintels, Sills, and Jambs:** Unless the masonry is self-supporting, brick veneer that is backed by wood or metal frame must be supported by lintels over openings. Concrete, cast stone, and stone lintels need to be the appropriate size in order to bear the weight of the veneer.
351	**16.2.2 Arches:** The following types are most commonly used for building arches: (Bullet #1 Only) ▪ ***Jack arch.*** A flat arch with zero or little rise.
398	**Figure 18-33.** Sheets of welded wire reinforcing are overlapped at least one full stay spacing plus 2."
444	**20.4.2 Exposed Aggregate:** Terrazzo toppings on outdoor slabs are generally ½" thick and contain marble, quartz, or granite chips.
518	**Glossary: tuckpointing.** Filling in the cut or defective mortar joints in masonry with fresh mortar. (10)

Modern Masonry
Tabs and Highlights

These 1 Exam Prep Tabs and Highlights are based on *Modern Masonry, 8th Edition*.

Each 1 Exam Prep Tabs sheet has five rows of tabs. Start with the first tab at the first row at the top of the page; proceed down that row placing the tabs at the locations listed below. Place each tab in your book setting it down one notch until you get to the bottom of a page. Then start back at the top again.

This concludes the tabs for this book. Please continue with the highlights on the following page.

A.M. 07/17/2020

Page	Highlight

5   **Figure 1-5.** C- Sled runner half round. D – Sled runner V groove

17   **Masonry Saws:** Blades are made of very hard material, such as silicon carbide or industrial diamond.

37   **Figure 3-4.** Symbols commonly found on construction drawings.

82 & 85   Learn the different types of building bricks and their uses. Also the difference between modular and non-modular brick.

91   **Solid Masonry Units:** A solid masonry unit is "one whose cross-sectional area in every plane parallel to the bearing surface is 75% or more of its gross cross-sectional area measured in the same plane."

These cored bricks are usually classified as solid masonry units because 75% of their area is solid material.

92   **Durability:** Several conditions affect weathering (durability) of a brick. These include heat, cold, and the action of soluble salts.

Figure 5-20. Efflorescence on masonry walls is caused by soluble salts in wet brick being carried to the surface as water evaporates.

96 & 97   **Five Basic Bonds:** Become familiar with the five basic bonds.

- Running bond
- Common bond or American bond
- Flemish bond: garden wall & double stretcher garden wall bond
- English bond: English cross or Dutch bond
- Block or stack bond

99   **Mortar Joints:** (4 Bullets)

- Concave joints
- V-shaped joints

Because the two joints are compacted, they effectively prevent rain from penetrating into the joint…The concave joint is the most popular mortar joint.

104   (FTX) unglazed facing tile:

- A high degree of mechanical perfection

119   **Figure 6-3.** Note: A **8x8x16** CMU (**sand and gravel**) weighs **40 lbs.**

122   **Sizes and Shapes:** Sizes are usually given in their nominal dimensions. A unit measuring 7 5/8" x 7 5/8" x 15 5/8" is known as a 8x8x16 unit.

125   The two-core design has the following advantages: (4 bullets)

133   **Glass Block:** Glass blocks are manufactured in three popular sizes…A ¼" mortar joint is required.

Figure 6-31

143   **Stone Applications:** Limestone is an excellent sill material that can be used on exterior masonry walls. The fact that it is one piece ensures better protection against water leakage.

| | |

BCSI: Building Component Safety Information 2018
Tabs and Highlights

These 1 Exam Prep tabs are based on *Building Component Safety Information: Guide to Good Practice for Handling, Installing, Restraining & Bracing of Metal Plate Connected Wood Trusses, 2018 (Updated 2020)*.

Each Tabs sheet has five rows of tabs. Start with the first tab at the first row at the top of the page, and proceed down that row placing the tabs at the locations listed below. Place each tab in your book setting it down one notch until you get to the bottom of the page, and then start back at the top again. After you have completed tabbing your book (the last tab is usually the glossary, appendix, or index), then you may start highlighting your book.

This concludes the tabs for this book. Please continue with the highlights on the following page.

A.M. 08/03/21

Page #	Highlight

Step 2. Determine the on-center spacing of Top Chord Temporary Lateral Restraint.

20

Step 3. Set first Truss (or Gable End Frame) and fasten securely to Ground Bracing verticals using minimum 2-16d nails at each junction and to the wall, or a directed by the Building Designer.

Step 4. Set Trusses 2,3,4 and 5 with TCTLR in line with Ground Bracing.

Step 5. Install Top Chord Diagonal Bracing.

Step 6. Install Web Member Plane Diagonal Bracing to stabilize the first five Trusses set (…).

Step 7. Install the Bottom Chord Temporary Lateral Restraint and Diagonal Bracing to stabilize the Bottom Chord plane(s).

Step 8. Continue the erection/installation process by installing the next four Trusses with the TCTLR and then repeating Steps 5, 6 and 7.

21

Table B2-1: Maximum Top Chord Temporary Lateral Restraint (TCTLR) Spacing Note: *Consult a Registered Design Professional for Trusses longer than 60'.

22

All Lateral Restraint and Diagonal Bracing material is at least 2 x 4 stress-graded lumber.

Figure B2-13 *Note: Maximum spacing for Top Chord Temporary Lateral Restraint *Highlight* **10' o.c. max*, 8' o.c. max*, 6' o.c. max*,** *and* **4' o.c. max***

24

Step 4: Set Trusses 2, 3, 4 and 5 with TCTLR in line with Ground Bracing: [Notice] Install Diagonal Bracing to the Top Chord plane immediately after the initial five Trusses have been set and restrained. Thereafter, install Diagonal Bracing to each subsequent set of four Trusses.

28

Step 8: Continue the Truss Installation Process Repeating Steps 4 through 7 with Groups of Fours Trusses using Option A or B below: [Caution] Remove only as much 2 x 4 Bracing as necessary to nail down the next sheet of Structural Sheathing.

33

Figure B2-49A

Figure B2-49B

35

Field Assembly & Other Special Conditions: Some Buildings are designed to have open ends (no end walls) or large door openings in the end walls. Apply Diagonal Bracing to the Bottom Chords between the rows of the Bottom Chord Lateral Restraint and at approximately 45º to the laterals. (See Figure B2-35).

36

Valley Set Frame Installation: The method used to frame a valley will affect how the Loads from the upper roof are distributed to the supporting Trusses…these Trusses are to be designed.

38

Table B3-1: Minimum Nail Size

Restraint/Bracing Materials & Fasteners: Use at least 2-10d (0.128x3"), 2-12d (0.128x3.25"), or 2-16d (0.131x3.5") nails to attach 2x4 Lateral Restraint and Diagonal Bracing members at each Connection as specified by the Truss Design or Building Designer. For 2 x 6 or greater Lateral Restraint and Diagonal Bracing, use a minimum of three nails per Connection.

41

Figure B3-11 *Highlight* Repeat Diagonal Bracing every 20' or as specified.

44

Always Diagonally Brace The Continuous Lateral Restraint!

Page #	Highlight

Page #   **Highlight**

49   **Figure B3-40 Note:** All Lateral Restraint and Diagonal Bracing material shall be a minimum of 2 x 4 Stress-graded Lumber.

53   **Table B4-1: Maximum Stack Height for Material on Trusses**

55   **Follow These Steps to Correct Damage, Jobsite Modifications or Installation Errors:** If a Truss is damaged, altered or improperly installed:

3. Do not attempt to repair the Truss without a Repair Detail from the Building Designer, Truss Designer or Truss Manufacturer.

59   **Common Installation Errors:** Spacing between rows of Top Chord Temporary Lateral Restraint (TCTLR) shall not exceed 10' on-center (oc) for 3 x 2 chords, and 15' oc for 4 x 2 chords.

Diagonal Bracing is critical and shall be installed at a maximum of every 15 Truss spaces or less.

60   **Installation Restraint/Bracing Requirements:** Bottom Chord Permanent Lateral Restraint shall be installed in rows not exceeding 10' oc or as directed by the Construction Documents or Building Designer.

Permanent Restraint & Bracing: Permanently restrain and brace the bottom chords of the PCT with directly applied gypsum board ceiling or with rows of lateral restraint installed at 10' on-center along the Truss span and diagonal bracing installed at no more than 20' intervals along the run of Trusses, unless otherwise specified.

65   **How Much Uplift and Lateral Resistance can Toe-Nailing Provide?** Table B8-1 provides the uplift and lateral Load capacities of Toe-nailed Connections consisting of three, four and five nails for various types of nails and species of wood.

Table B8-1: Uplift and Lateral Resistance Capacity of Toe-Nailed Connections Attaching Truss to Double Top Plate of Wall

77   **Temporary Installation Restraint/Bracing Principles:**

Step 1: Ensure Stable Side Wall and End Wall Columns

Step 2: Provide A Stable Base Unit Upon Which to Build

78   **Step 3: Temporary Restraint/Bracing of The Truss Base Unit**

79   **Table B10-1: Maximum Truss Spans for Top Chord size, grade and spacing between rows of Lateral Restraint.**

The Top Chord Temporary Lateral Restraint spacing schedules in Table B10-1 were developed for an assumed Load consisting of the weight of the Truss, plus two 250 lb workers (…).

80   Install rows of Bottom Chord Temporary Lateral Restraint (BCTLR) at a maximum of 15' oc.

Bottom Chord **Permanent** Lateral Restraint shall be installed at no more than 10' oc.

89   **Fall Protection & Trusses:** "Each employee engaged in residential construction activities 6 feet or more above lower levels shall be protected by…net system or a personal fall arrest system."

96   **Qualified Person:** Under [OSHA 29 CFR 1926.503(a)(2)], a qualified person is one who should have knowledge, and be able to provide training…the role of employees in fall protection plans."

1 Exam Prep
BCSI-Building Component Safety Information
Guide to Good Practice for Handling, Installing, Restraining & Bracing of Metal Plate Connected Wood Trusses
Tabs and Highlights

These 1 Exam Prep tabs are based on *BCSI- Guide to Good Practice for Handling, Installing, Restraining & Bracing of Metal Plate Connected Wood Trusses, 2013 Edition*.

Each 1 Exam Prep tabs sheet has five rows of tabs. Start with the first tab at the first row at the top of the page; proceed down that row placing the tabs at the locations listed below. Place each tab in your book setting it down one notch until you get to the last tab (usually the index or glossary). Then start with the highlights.

This concludes the tabs for this book. Please continue with the highlights below.

Section #	Highlight

Gypsum Construction Handbook, Seventh Edition
Tabs and Highlights

These 1 Exam Prep tabs are based on *The Gypsum Construction Handbook, Seventh Edition.*

Each Tabs sheet has five rows of tabs. Start with the first tab at the first row at the top of the page, and proceed down that row placing the tabs at the locations listed below. Place each tab in your book setting it down one notch until you get to the bottom of the page, and then start back at the top again. After you have completed tabbing your book (the last tab is usually the glossary, appendix, or index), then you may start highlighting your book.

*** *This concludes the tabs for this book. Please continue with the highlights below.* ***

Carpentry and Building Construction
Questions and Answers

1. _____ are groups of related occupations.

   A. Career pathways
   B. Career clusters
   C. Occupation set
   D. Career set

2. The purpose of _____ is/are to ensure that building are structurally sound and safe from fire and other hazards.

   A. OSHA
   B. Stock plans
   C. Surveys
   D. Building codes

3. A _____ is a scale drawing showing the size and location of rooms on a given floor.

   A. Stock plan
   B. Blueprint
   C. Floor plan
   D. Schedule

4. Bulkhead is more commonly known as _____.

   A. Soffit
   B. Chase
   C. Cornice
   D. Eave

5. In concrete walls a cold joint occurs when _____.

   A. Concrete batches are mixed differently
   B. Fresh concrete poured on top of or next to concrete that has already begun to cure
   C. Too much air is in the concrete
   D. There is too much moisture in the concrete and the temperature is below 30°F

6. _____ is the measuring system used by the United States.

    A. Customary
    B. Metric
    C. Standard
    D. Both A and C

7. A scale of _____ is the most often used for drawing houses.

    A. 1/8" = 1'0"
    B. ¼" = 1'0"
    C. ½" = 1'0"
    D. 1/2" = 2'0"

8. A _____ is a large landing at the top of steps.

    A. Stoop
    B. Porch
    C. Deck
    D. Large – scale landing

9. A tile without glaze is called _____.

    A. Unfinished
    B. Matte
    C. Bisque
    D. None of the above

10. In dealing with wood basics, a cambium _____.

    A. The rings of the tree that make give it its grain appearance
    B. Layer of living tissue that produces sapwood
    C. The fibers of the tree that gives it its hardness
    D. None of the above

11. _____ is not identified by a softwood board's grade stamp.

    A. Species
    B. Moisture content
    C. Price per lineal ft.
    D. Mill number

12. The horizontal part of a step upon which the foot is placed is called the _____.

    A. Riser
    B. Nosing
    C. Tread
    D. Baluster

13. OSB stands for _____.

    A. Occupational Safety Board
    B. Optimal-strand board
    C. Oriented-strand board
    D. Open-steel beam

14. The _____ is the part of a window that holds the glazing.

    A. Muntin
    B. Sash
    C. Casing
    D. Mounting flange

15. The _____ is the overall size of the window, including casings.

    A. Nominal dimension
    B. Total window dimension (TWD)
    C. Actual dimension
    D. Unit dimension

16. _____ are written notes that may be arranged in list form.

    A. Schedules
    B. Specifications
    C. Engineering renderings
    D. Site details

17. The abbreviation MH stands for _____ in estimating.

    A. Man hours
    B. Middle-hand
    C. Materials holding
    D. Monetary holding

18. _____ is another name for overhead.

    A. Fixed costs
    B. Indirect costs
    C. Static costs
    D. None of the above

19. In concrete, crazing is _____.

    A. Another name for moist curing the concrete
    B. Whitest crystalline deposits that sometimes appears on the surface of the concrete
    C. Appearance of fine cracks that appear in irregular patterns over the surface of the concrete
    D. The formation of loose powder on the surface of hardening concrete

20. A _____ test is a test to measure the consistency of concrete.

    A. Slump
    B. Moisture
    C. Cube
    D. Viscosity

21. _____ footings are often used on a lot that slopes.

    A. Pier
    B. Rabbeted
    C. Monolithic
    D. Stepped

22. A _____ is a transit that reads horizontal and vertical angles electronically.

    A. Vernier scale
    B. Theodolite
    C. Electronic transit level
    D. Electronic layout device

23. _____ is the process of spreading mortar or cement plaster over the block wall.

    A. Troweling
    B. Leveling
    C. Parging
    D. Grading

24. A glue laminated beam is often called a _____.

    A. Camber
    B. Spline
    C. Glulam
    D. Gambrel

25. The _____ of a door refers to the direction in which a door will swing.

I. Lock face
II. Hinge face
III. Hand

    A. III
    B. II
    C. I
    D. I and II

26. 3 ½" represents _____ feet on a ¼" scale.

    A. 10
    B. 12
    C. 14
    D. 16

27. On a blueprint, lines that terminate with arrows are _____ lines.

    A. Dimension
    B. Center
    C. Leader
    D. Break

28. The _____ plan shows the building with boundaries.

    A. Foundation
    B. Plot or site
    C. Floor
    D. Framing

29. The _____ plan shows window and door placement.

    A. Foundation
    B. Plot or site
    C. Framing
    D. Floor

30. The _____ plan shows the external views of the structure.

    A. Elevation
    B. Plot or site
    C. Foundation
    D. Framing

31. When precise information is needed about a small or complex portion of the building, you would look for _____ on a plan.

    A. Section views
    B. A detail drawing
    C. Engineering drawings
    D. Mechanical plan

32. The _____ on the blueprint designates the brand and model number of a window.

    A. Section views
    B. A detail drawing
    C. Window schedule
    D. Elevation

33. Concrete mixture is made of _____.

    I. Cement
    II. Sand
    III. Gravel
    IV. Water

        A. II and IV
        B. II and III
        C. II, III, & IV
        D. I, II, III & IV

34. _____ impacts the weight of concrete the most.

        A. Silt
        B. Aggregate
        C. Water
        D. None of the above

35. _____ admixtures are added to concrete to make it set up at a slower rate.

        A. Air-Entraining
        B. Super-Plasticizing
        C. Retarding
        D. Water-reducing

36. Concrete gains most of its strength in the _____ day period after it has been placed.

        A. 28
        B. 14
        C. 7
        D. 30

37. To remove air pockets from concrete _____ is performed.

        A. A slump test
        B. Moist curing
        C. Crazing
        D. Consolidation

38. #5 rebar is _____ inch thick.

        A. 3/8
        B. 5/8
        C. 1/8
        D. None of the above

39. A _____ measures horizontal angles only.

    A. Level
    B. Builder's square
    C. Protractor
    D. Transit

40. When laying out a building, what is the starting point from which measurements can be made?

    I. Benchmark
    II. Point of reference
    III. Station mark

    A. II
    B. I and III
    C. I and II
    D. III

41. A _____ is a board fastened horizontally to stakes placed to the outside where the corners of the building will be located.

    A. Corner board
    B. Batter board
    C. Starter strip
    D. Foundation board

42. _____ is a measure of how well the soil can support the weight of a house.

    A. Load capacity
    B. Bearing capacity
    C. Load resistance
    D. None of the above

43. The minimum distance from the point of excavation that batter boards can be placed is _____ feet.

    A. 2
    B. 3
    C. 4
    D. 5

44. In surveying, if rod "A" reads 4' and rod "B" reads 4'6", then _____.

    A. The ground point of "B" is 6" higher than the ground point of "A".
    B. The ground point of "A" is 6" lower than the ground point of "B".
    C. The ground point of "A" is 6" higher than the ground point of "B".
    D. None of the above

45. The formula for estimating concrete in cubic yards is _____.

    A. L x W x D ÷ 12
    B. L x W x D ÷ 27
    C. L x W x D ÷ 26
    D. L x W x D ÷ 24

46. The sides of footings are molded by boards referred to as _____ boards.

    A. Batter
    B. Backer
    C. Haunch
    D. Form

47. A _____ clip is used to hold foundation wall forms together.

    A. Snap ties
    B. Bracket
    C. 6d nails
    D. Wales

48. In constructing a stack bond pattern block wall, what additional step is required that is NOT needed wit a common bond wall?

    A. Joints should be tooled smooth to seal them against water seepage
    B. Joint reinforcement must be added to every third course
    C. Joint reinforcement must be added to every second course
    D. Full bedding should be performed

49. A _____ support is used over window and door openings in a concrete block wall.

    A. Lintel
    B. Girder
    C. Collar beam
    D. Bond beam

50. A standard mortar joint when using concrete block is _____ inch wide.

    A. 1/8
    B. ¼
    C. 3/8
    D. 5/8

51. _____ is the nominal size of a standard block. Choose the closest answer.

    A. 6" x 6" x 14"
    B. 7" x 8 x 16"
    C. 7" x 7" x 15"
    D. 8" x 8" x 16"

52. Mortar should be used within _____ hours when the air temperature is 80°F or higher.

    A. 1 ½
    B. 2
    C. 2 ½
    D. 3 ½

53. A _____ is a horizontal member placed at the bottom of a window opening to support the window.

    A. Trimmer stud
    B. Rough sill
    C. Cripple stud
    D. Stool

54. The curve or camber on glulam beams should be installed with the curve oriented _____.

    A. Up, toward the ceiling
    B. Underneath, toward the floor
    C. In the direction opposite the fastener
    D. None of the above

55. Lumber shrinks, but, is most troublesome when shrinkage occurs across the _____ of a board.

    A. Length
    B. Width
    C. Height
    D. None of the above

56. A common defect in lumber where a lengthwise grain separation occurs through the growth ring is known as _____.

    A. Knot
    B. Pitch
    C. Ring Shake
    D. Torn grain

57. The type of wood with lowest resistance to decay is _____.

    A. Redwood
    B. Heartwood of bald cypress
    C. Cedar
    D. Sapwood of all common native wood

58. If a sheet of plywood has a 32/16 panel identification index, it may be used as a floor decking with a maximum span of _____ inches.

    A. 32
    B. 16
    C. 24
    D. None of the above

59. Plywood that is used for concrete forms must, at minimum, be grade _____.

    A. C-D
    B. A-C
    C. B-B
    D. A-B

60. Horizontal members that carry the heaviest load of attached horizontal members are called _____

    A. Girders
    B. Floor joist
    C. Collar beam
    D. Lally columns

61. When laying plywood subfloor, the spacing between each of the panels is _____ inch on ends and sides.

    A. 1/8
    B. 1/4
    C. 5/6
    D. 3/6

62. The main support under a wood deck is called a _____.

    A. Post
    B. Sill plate
    C. Floor joist
    D. Girder

63. A built-up girder should have _____ inches of clearance between the end of the girder and the masonry in a masonry pocket.

    A. 1/8
    B. ½
    C. ¼
    D. 1/16

64. If the run of the standard rafter is 12 feet, the run of the king hip is _____ feet. Select closest answer.

    A. 15
    B. 16
    C. 17
    D. 18

65. _____ doors consist of stiles and rails.

    A. Flat-panel
    B. Raised panel
    C. Solid-core construction
    D. Sliding

66. The standard height of an interior door is _____.

    A. 6'8" or 7'0"
    B. 6'6" or 6'8"
    C. 6'4" or 6'6"
    D. 7'0" or 7'2"

67. The proper way to hang a bifold door is _____.

    A. Install the top track, install the door, the install the bottom track
    B. Install the bottom track first, then fasten the top track to the ceiling
    C. Install the top track first, then fasten the lower track to the floor directly under the top rack.
    D. None of the above

68. The door hinge size for a 1- 3/8" interior door is _____.

    A. 3" x 3 ½"
    B. 2 ½ x 2 ½"
    C. 3" x 3"
    D. 3 ½" x 3 ½"

69. When installing a door stop, nail the stop on the _____ side first.

    A. Hinge
    B. Lock
    C. It does not matter which side
    D. Depends if it is a right or left hand door

70. When installing plywood soffit to the ledger strip, nails should be installed _____ inches apart.

    A. 2
    B. 4
    C. 6
    D. 8

71. One square of 235-pound shingles will cover _____ square feet and weigh _____ pounds.

    A. 100; 235
    B. 50; 100
    C. 175; 235
    D. 200; 200

72. The typical exposure while using roll roofing is _____ inches.

    A. 15
    B. 16
    C. 17
    D. 19

73. Roll roofing end laps should be offset _____ inches.

    A. 4
    B. 6
    C. 7
    D. 8

74. When using roll roofing, the strip should be nailed so that it overhangs the edge by a minimum of _____ inch.

    A. ¼
    B. ½
    C. 1/8
    D. 3/16

75. The proper installation of drip edge calls for it to be installed _____.

    A. It is applied to the fascia and under the underlayment at the eaves, but over the underlayment at the rake
    B. It is applied to the sheathing and under the underlayment at the rake, but over the underlayment at the eaves
    C. It is applied to the sheathing and under the underlayment at the eaves, but over the underlayment at the rake
    D. None of the above

76. There are _____ bundles of shingles in a square of roofing.

    A. Two
    B. Three
    C. Four
    D. Five

77. When installing shingles, no nails should be placed within _____ inches of a valley.

    A. 2
    B. 4
    C. 6
    D. 8

78. Gutters are fastened to the _____ of a house.

    A. Soffit
    B. Roof eave
    C. Gable end
    D. Fascia

79. Splash blocks at the bottom of drain spouts should be at least _____ foot/feet long.

    A. 3
    B. 2
    C. 1
    D. None of the above

80. The minimum overlap for 6 inches beveled lap siding is _____ inch(es).

    A. 1
    B. 1.25
    C. 1.5
    D. 1.75

81. The ends of siding boards cut during installation should be coated with _____.

    A. Same color paint as the siding
    B. Water repellant
    C. Rustoleum
    D. Termite shield

82. The strip nailed to the end of the rafter is _____.

    A. Starter strip
    B. Fascia
    C. Frieze
    D. Ventilator

83. _____ are used at the brick course below the bottom of the sheathing and framing.

    A. Girders
    B. Floor joists
    C. Flashing
    D. Brick veneer

84. Radiating stair treads are also known as _____.

    A. Landings
    B. Newels
    C. Risers
    D. Winders

85. The horizontal length of a stairway is called _____.

    A. Total run
    B. Total rise
    C. Unit rise
    D. Unit run

86. The total rise for a stairway is 8'-11". The total amount of risers in the stairway is _____.

    A. 13
    B. 14
    C. 15
    D. 16

87. A stair stringer must have _____ inches remaining after it has been notched.

    A. 2
    B. 2 ½
    C. 3
    D. 3 ½

88. A third stair stringer should be installed in the middle of the stairs when the stair width exceeds _____.

    A. 2'0"
    B. 2'4"
    C. 2'6"
    D. 2' 8"

89. A standard kitchen base cabinet, not including the countertop, is _____ inches tall.

    A. 34
    B. 34 ½
    C. 36
    D. 38

90. A standard kitchen wall cabinet is _____ inches deep.

    A. 10
    B. 12
    C. 14
    D. 18

91. A standard kitchen base cabinet is _____ inches deep.

    A. 18
    B. 20
    C. 24
    D. 28

92. When installing ¾" thick cabinets to studs covered with ½" drywall, the screws should be _____ to fasten the cabinets to the wall.

    A. 2 ¼" or long enough to go through the ¾ back rail and wall covering and extend at least 2" into the studs
    B. 2 ¼" or long enough to go through the ¾ back rail and wall covering and extend at least 1" into the studs
    C. 2 1/2" or long enough to go through the ¼ back rail and wall covering and extend at least 1" into the studs
    D. None of the above

93. A contractor is installing wall cabinets in a new home built with 2 x 6 studs. Some of the cabinets span only a single stud. The cabinets are attached with _____.

    A. Two #10 screws into the single stud and at least two 3/16" x 3 ½" toggle bolts through the drywall.
    B. Four #10 screws into the single stud and at least two 3/16" x 3 ½" toggle bolts through the drywall.
    C. Two #10 screws into the single stud and at least two 5/16" x 3 ½" toggle bolts through the drywall.
    D. None of the above

94. Wood flooring should be stored in the building in which it is going to be installed in for _____ to allow for acclimation.

    A. At least 3 days
    B. At least 4 days
    C. At least 7 days
    D. 14 days

95. The first board of tongue and groove flooring should be installed _____ inches from the frame wall and with the _____ end of the board facing the wall.

    A. 1/4" to 5/8"; Tongue
    B. 1/2" to 5/8"; Tongue
    C. 1/2" to 5/8"; Grooved
    D. 1/2" to 3/8"; Grooved

96. _____ is used as a base for tile and in shower stalls.

    A. Backerboard
    B. Sheathing
    C. Plywood
    D. Fiberglass

97. _____ is NOT a common unit of measure.

    A. Length
    B. Liquid
    C. Volume
    D. Weight

98. Cracks in lumber that run parallel to and between the annular rings are called _____.

    A. Crooks
    B. Cracks
    C. Shakes
    D. Splits

99. A board measures 6' long, 10" wide and 2" thick. _____ board feet of lumber are contained in th_ board.

    A. 0
    B. 10
    C. 1.3
    D. 15

100. _____ is not true of plywood.

    A. Face and cross band are in the same direction
    B. There are always an odd number of piles
    C. Grain in outside layers runs in the same direction
    D. Grain in successive plies runs at right angles

101. The best appearing face veneer' of a softwood plywood panel is indicated by the letter _____.

    A. A
    B. B
    C. E
    D. N

102. Panels made from reconstituted wood bonded with adhesive under heat and pressure are known as _____.

    A. Wafer board
    B. OSB
    C. Hard board
    D. All of the above

103. Engineered lumber products are designed as replacements or substitutes for _____.

    A. Solid lumber
    B. Second growth lumber
    C. Steel framing
    D. Structural lumber

104. Laminated veneer lumber is manufactured in lengths up to _____ feet.

    A. 30
    B. 40
    C. 50
    D. 66

105. The tool most commonly used to lay out or test angles other than those laid out with squares is called a _____.

    A. Sliding T-bevel
    B. Compass
    C. Protractor
    D. Caliper

106. The saw commonly used with a miter box is called a _____.

    A. Cross-saw
    B. Rip-saw
    C. Back-saw
    D. Hack-saw

107. The size of a claw hammer is determined by _____.

    A. Length of the claw
    B. Overall dimension
    C. Weight of the entire hammer
    D. Weight of the head

108. To bore holes over one inch in diameter, the carpenter uses a (an) _____.

    A. Auger bit
    B. Bit brace
    C. Expansion bit
    D. Hole saw

109. A _____ cut, is a type of mitre cut that is made through the thickness of a board

    A. Bevel
    B. Mitre
    C. Coping
    D. Chamfer

110. A level transit differs from a builder's level in that it _____.

    A. Can traverse a 360° horizontal angle
    B. Can measure vertical angles
    C. Has a Vernier scale
    D. Has four leveling screws

111. A _____ is a mark on a permanent fixed object from which measurements and elevations are taken.

    A. Turning point
    B. Station
    C. Reference
    D. Benchmark

112. The point of reference where the builder's level is located is called the _____.

    A. Degree mark
    B. Benchmark
    C. Elevation mark
    D. Station mark

113. Batter boards should be set a minimum of _____ feet outside the building lines and in such a manner that they will not be disturbed during excavation and construction.

    A. 4
    B. 6
    C. 5
    D. 10

114. One of the advantages of the balloon frame is that _____.

    A. The bottom plates act as fire stops
    B. There is little shrinkage in the frame
    C. The second-floor joists rest on a ribbon instead of a plate
    D. It is stronger, stiffer and more resistant to lateral pressures

115. A system of framing where the floor joists of each story rest on the top of the plates of the story below _____ is called framing.

    A. Stud
    B. Balloon
    C. Platform
    D. Post and beam

116. You usually find "ribbons" in _____ construction.

    A. Post and beam
    B. Balloon framing
    C. Platform Framing
    D. Any of the above

117. A large horizontal beam that supports the inner ends of floor joists is called a _____.

    A. Pier
    B. Girder
    C. Stud
    D. Sill

118. _____ is not a commonly available wood beam or girder.

    A. Solid Wood beam
    B. Laminate beam
    C. Glue Laminate
    D. Built up

119. Ten 2'L x 12" W X 16H" board contain _____ board feet of lumber.

    A. 240
    B. 320
    C. 267
    D. 400

120. The top and bottom horizontal members of a wall frame are called _____.

    A. Headers
    B. Plates
    C. Trimmers
    D. Sills

121. The horizontal wall member supporting the load over an opening is called a _____.

    A. Header
    B. Rough sill
    C. Plate
    D. Truss

122. When framing a pre-hung door unit that has a 36" door, the width of the rough opening would be _____.

    A. 38"
    B. 40"
    C. The width of the unit plus 1/2"
    D. The width of the unit plus 1"

123. A birds mouth is a notch cut in a rafter to fit it to the _____.

    A. Fascia
    B. Ridge
    C. Soffit
    D. Plate

124. A member of the cornice generally fastened to the rafter tails is called the _____.

    A. Drip
    B. Fascia
    C. Plancher
    D. Soffit

125. A window that consists of an upper and lower sash that slides vertically is called a _____ window.

    A. Casement
    B. Double-hung
    C. Hopper
    D. Sliding

126. Stairways in residential construction should have a minimum width of _____ inches.

    A. Thirty
    B. Thirty-two
    C. Thirty-six
    D. Forty

127. Most building codes specify a minimum headroom clearance of _____ .

    A. 6'6"
    B. 6' 8"
    C. 7'0"
    D. 7'6"

Please see Answer Key on the following page
3/14/23

Carpentry and Building Construction
Questions and Answers
Answer Key

Answer	Page #	
B	6	
D	34	
C	37	
A	460	
B	266	
D	42	
B	44	
A	1018	
C	990	
B	318	
C	324	
C	725	
C	349	
B	577	
D	586	
B	57	
A	61	Table 2-2 Common Abbreviations Used in Estimating
B	64	
C	222	
A	226	
D	259	
B	238	
C	287	
C	360	
A	601	
C	44	

Scale is ¼" to 1 ft

¼"/1ft = 3 ½"/x

x = 3 ½ / ¼

x = 3.5/.25

x = 14 feet

A	45
B	50
D	51
A	53

	Answer	**Page #**
31.	B	55
32.	C	56
33.	D	218
34.	B	220
35.	C	221
36.	A	223
37.	D	227
38.	B	230
39.	A	237
40.	C	239
41.	B	244
42.	B	247
43.	C	244 – 245
44.	C	246
45.	B	250, 266
46.	C	258
47.	A	265
48.	C	277
49.	A	287
50.	C	275
51.	D	275
52.	C	279
53.	B	434
54.	A	361
55.	B	323
56.	C	326
57.	D	329
58.	B	341
59.	C	341
60.	A	396
61.	A	421, 423
62.	D	396
63.	B	401
64.	C	506
65.	B	597
66.	A	615
67.	C	616
68.	D	619
69.	B	620
70.	C	557
71.	A	626
72.	C	629
73.	B	629

	Answer	Page #
4.	A	629
5.	C	634
6.	B	637
7.	C	641
8.	D	651
9.	A	653
0.	A	663
1.	B	663
2.	B	552
3.	C	698
4.	D	730
5.	A	732
6.	C	734	Step-by-step application
7.	D	737
8.	C	736
9.	B	784
0.	B	783
1.	C	784
2.	B	796
3.	A	797
4.	B	975
5.	C	979
6.	A	993
7.	B	42
8.	C	326
9.	B	63
00.	A	338
01.	A	340
02.	B	349
03.	A	352
04.	D	353
05.	A	110
06.	C	113
07.	D	118
08.	A	166
09.	A	136
10.	B	238
11.	D	239
12.	D	239
13.	A	244
14.	B	370
15.	B	370
16.	B	370

	Answer	**Page #**
117.	B	396
118.	A	398
119.	B	63
		2 x 12 x 16 = 384
		384 / 12 = 32
		32 x 10 = 320
120.	B	432
121.	A	432
122.	A	432
123.	D	481
124.	B	552
125.	B	578
126.	C	730
127.	B	730

The Contractors Guide to Quality Concrete Construction, 4th Ed.
Questions and Answers

The most common type of cement is Type _____ .

A.   I
B.   II
C.   III
D.   IV

High-early-strength cement is Type _____ .

A.   II
B.   III
C.   IV
D.   V

Low heat-of-hydration cement is Type _____ .

A.   II
B.   III
C.   IV
D.   V

Test cylinders stored on the job would ideally be stored under what conditions?

A.   Controlled moisture
B.   Controlled temperature
C.   Controlled conditions
D.   All of the above

What is not an example of a pozzolan?

A.   Microsilica
B.   Class C Fly Ash
C.   Class F Fly Ash
D.   Granulated slag

A_____ is used to extend the setting time of concrete in hot water.

A.   Accelerator
B.   Retarder
C.   Extending agents
D.   Setting inhibitor

7.   _____ accelerates the setting of concrete but is prohibited in pre-stressed concrete designs.

    A.   Calcium chloride
    B.   Fly ash
    C.   Calcium hypochlorite
    D.   Sodium bicarbonate

8.   For hot-weather concreting, a maximum concrete delivery temperature of _____° F is often specified.

    A.   80
    B.   75
    C.   95
    D.   90

9.   You can increase the slump of concrete 5 to 7 inches by adding a/an _____ .

    A.   Retarder
    B.   Superplasticizer
    C.   Accelerator
    D.   Aggregate

10.   To what depth should a control joint be cut into a concrete slab?

    A.   One-eight the slab thickness
    B.   One-fourth the slab thickness
    C.   10% of the slab thickness
    D.   up to 60% of the slab thickness

11.   What is/are the fiber material(s) in fiber-reinforced concrete?

    A.   Glass
    B.   Steel
    C.   Polypropylene
    D.   All of the above

12.   In _____ splice, the bars are lapped next to each other at a certain length and securely wired together with tie wire.

    A.   Lap
    B.   Welded
    C.   Mechanical
    D.   None of the above

13.   For concrete cast against and permanently exposed to earth (such as footings), minimum cover for bundled bars is _____.

    A.   1 inch
    B.   2 inches
    C.   3 inches
    D.   4 inches

4. What type of wire is used to tie rebars?

   A. No. 16 gage black soft annealed wire
   B. No. 14 gage soft annealed wire
   C. No. 16 gage green annealed wire
   D. No. 12 gage annealed wire

5. What type of tie is used to secure heavy mats of rebars to be lifted in place by a crane?

   A. Type A
   B. Type B
   C. Type C
   D. Type D

6. What is the maximum distance for placing control joints in a wall without openings?

   A. 18 feet
   B. 20 feet
   C. 24 feet
   D. 25 feet

7. Contraction joints in floors are designed _____ .

   A. To control random cracking
   B. So a crack forms at a pre-selected location
   C. To provide a deliberately weakened plane
   D. All of the above

8. Control joints in slabs on grade are made by cutting into the slab to a depth of _____ times the slab thickness on the first cut.

   A. 1/8
   B. 1/4
   C. 1/2
   D. 3/4

9. In an eight inch (8") slab, control joints should be placed every _____ feet.

   A. 16
   B. 18
   C. 20
   D. 24

10. What is an isolation joint?

   A. A joint made to accommodate movements cause by temperature changes
   B. A joint used at a point of restraint, including the junction between the elements of a structure
   C. A joint located where one placement ends and the next one begins
   D. None of the above

21. The <u>basic raw</u> materials of Portland cement are:

    A.   limestone, clay or shale
    B.   calcium, silica, iron
    C.   alumina, limestone, clay
    D.   alumina, calcium, shale

22. Reinforcing wire in slabs should be placed _____ inch(es) from the top of the slab.

    A.   1
    B.   1.5
    C.   2
    D.   2.5

23. What procedure is used to prevent excessive absorption of water from concrete slabs on grade?

    A.   Before concreting, moisten the subgrade
    B.   Before concreting, saturate the subgrade
    C.   Use of a high-range water reducer
    D.   None of the above

24. Joints in concrete should be sawcut within how many hours?

    A.   Within 2 to 8 hours
    B.   Within 4 to 10 hours
    C.   Within 4 to 12 hours
    D.   Within 6 to 18 hours

25. When concrete placement is interrupted, what type of joint must be provided?

    A.   A construction joint
    B.   A warping joint
    C.   An isolation joint
    D.   None of the above

26. When floating air-entrained concrete the bullfloat should be made of what material?

    I.   Aluminum
    II.   Magnesium
    III.   Zinc

    A.   I and II
    B.   II and III
    C.   I only
    D.   II only

7. What is used to embed course aggregate particles into the slab?

   A. Checkrod
   B. Vibratory screed
   C. Power float
   D. Wood float

8. After non-air-entrained concrete is screeded it should be floated with a _____ .

   A. Wood float
   B. Aluminum float
   C. Magnesium float
   D. None of the above

9. When should finish troweling begin?

   A. Just before the water sheen disappears
   B. After the water sheen has disappeared
   C. Immediately after screeding
   D. None of the above

10. When using a vibrator on concrete, it should not be kept in one location more than _____ .

   A. 1 minute
   B. 10 to 15 seconds
   C. 20 to 30 seconds
   D. 30 to 45 seconds

. The maximum height from which a concrete mixture (not specifically designed to prevent segregation) can be dropped without segregation is _____ feet.

   A. 2
   B. 10
   C. 8
   D. 4

. Spreading rocks on the surface of a slab and pressing them into the surface is which technique of creating an exposed aggregate finish?

   A. Monolithic technique
   B. Seeding technique
   C. Exposing technique
   D. All of the above

. Cold weather concreting procedures are required if the average temperature falls below _____° F.

   A. 60
   B. 50
   C. 40
   D. 30

34. What is the purpose for installing welded wire mesh in a concrete slab?

   A. To prevent cracks from opening
   B. To increase-load carrying capacity
   C. To add flexural strength
   D. None of the above

35. A non-skid surface on outdoor slabs is created with a _____ .

   A. Stiff broom
   B. Texture trowel
   C. Soft broom
   D. None of the above

36. Low humidity and wind are the primary causes of rapidly evaporating surface moisture that causes the surface tension resulting in _____ .

   A. Shrinkage cracks
   B. Crazing
   C. Plastic shrinkage cracks
   D. Blistering

37. Sealing the surface of the concrete before it is fully compacted causes_____ .

   A. Shrinkage cracks
   B. Crazing
   C. Plastic shrinkage cracks
   D. Blistering

38. Test cylinders stored on the job site should be protected from drying and maintained at a temperature _____ range.

   A. 50 to 70° F
   B. 55 to 75° F
   C. 60 to 80° F
   D. 65 to 85° F

39. What procedure is used to prevent segregation of concrete components when pouring a slab?

   A. The concrete should be spread as it is deposited
   B. Deposit the concrete in a pile and then spread with a vibrator
   C. Addition of an admixture
   D. None of the above

40. When performing a slump test, each layer is rodded _____ times.

   A. 10
   B. 15
   C. 25
   D. 50

. The normal curing time for formed concrete is _____ .

A. 12 to 48 hours
B. 12 to 72 hours
C. 48 to 72 hours
D. None of the above

. Excessive bleeding can be caused by _____.

A. too much fly ash in the mixture
B. not enough mixture water
C. over vibration
D. excess mixture water and insufficient fines in mixture

. Saw-cutting joints should be done within _____ hours of concrete placement.

A. 1 to 2
B. 2 to 6
C. 4 to 10
D. 4 to 12

. The maximum delivery time for ready-mixed concrete is _____ minutes.

A. 30
B. 60
C. 90
D. 120

. 1 gallon of water added to a cubic yard of concrete will increase slump _____ inch.

A. ¼
B. ½
C. 1
D. 2

. Concrete cylinder tests are used to _____.

A. estimate concrete strength at a given time
B. determine the workability if the mix
C. see if the mix segregates
D. see how much the concrete expands

. When you need concrete to set quickly, what type of concrete should be used to produce high early strength?

A. Type I
B. Type II
C. Type III
D. Type IV

48. What chemical reaction takes place when portland cement is hardening?

   A. Permeability
   B. Hydration
   C. Dehydration
   D. None of the above

49. What is the effect of adding too much water to concrete?

   A. Lower slump, higher strength
   B. Lower slump, lower strength
   C. Higher slump, lower strength
   D. Higher slump, higher strength

50. What is the difference between fine & coarse aggregate?

   A. The coarse stone will not pass through a 1/4" sieve
   B. The coarse stone will not pass through a 1/8" sieve
   C. The coarse stone will not pass through a 1/16" sieve
   D. None of the above

51. What should be added to concrete in cold weather?

   A. Calcium hypochlorite
   B. Calcium chloride
   C. Sodium bicarbonate
   D. Fly ash

52. Which of the following is NOT a reason to use an admixture?

   A. To increase early strength
   B. To increase permeability
   C. To increase ultimate strength
   D. To increase workability

53. What is not true of air-entrained concrete?

   A. Increased workability
   B. Segregation is reduced
   C. It is essential to durability
   D. Must be used for interior flatwork

54. What is the effect of adding too much water to a concrete mix?

   A. Higher slump, lower strength
   B. Higher slump, higher strength
   C. Lower slump, lower strength
   D. Lower slump, higher strength

What is the proper location of welded wire mesh in a concrete slab?

A. 1" below the slab surface, in the upper half of the slab
B. 1.5" below the slab surface, in the upper third of the slab
C. 2" below the slab surface, in the upper third of the slab
D. 2" below the slab surface, in the upper half of the slab

The maximum delivery time for ready mix concrete after water has been added to the cement is _____ .

A. 30 minutes
B. 60 minutes
C. 120 minutes
D. 90 minutes

Mat or floating foundations are specified when _____ .

A. Budget does not allow for additional cost
B. When builder is looking for a more economical choice
C. The allowable bearing capacity of the soil is very low to great depths
D. None of the above

What type of forms are used to place concrete by extrusion?

A. Slipforms
B. Jump forms
C. Stay-in-place forms
D. All of the above

What is the minimal quality plywood that can be used when building concrete forms?

A. A-B
B. B-B
C. A-A
D. A-C

A concrete containing a lightweight aggregate should be presoaked to 70 to 80 % total absorption. If not, it will _____ .

A. Segregate
B. Crack when it dries
C. Make pumping more difficult
D. Lose moisture quickly

Which of the following is the most economical wood to use for formwork?

A. Cedar
B. Kiln-dried pine
C. Mahogany
D. Oak

62. The working load of new ties used in formwork should have a safety factor of _____ .

    A.   2:1
    B.   2:2
    C.   3:1
    D.   1:2

63. The purpose for form liners is to provide _____ on concrete surfaces.

    A.   Designs
    B.   Patterns
    C.   Textures
    D.   All of the above

64. How much does concrete weigh per cubic foot?

    A.   100 lbs.
    B.   125 lbs.
    C.   150 lbs.
    D.   200 lbs.

65. What is the best way to reduce lateral pressure on concrete forms when placing concrete?

    A.   Slower placement or rate of pour
    B.   Faster placement or rate of pour
    C.   Distributing concrete as it pours out
    D.   None of the above

66. When an engineer's specifications for removal of concrete forms is not available, the ACI has recommendations for the length of time concrete should remain in the forms when the air temperature is above _____.

    A.   45° F
    B.   50° F
    C.   60° F
    D.   65° F

67. What is the main reason for steel reinforcement in a concrete member?

    A.   To increase compressive strength
    B.   To reduce cracking over time
    C.   To resist tensile forces
    D.   None of the above

68. Placing drawings show details for fabrication and _____ .

    A.   Formwork
    B.   Placing concrete
    C.   Placing of reinforcing steel
    D.   None of the above

What are the characteristics of a #5 bar?

A. .325" diameter .20% area 1.022 lbs. per lineal foot
B. .425" diameter .21% area 1.033 lbs. per lineal foot
C. .525" diameter .31% area 1.032 lbs. per lineal foot
D. .625" diameter .31% area 1.043 lbs. per lineal foot

What do the markings on rebar represent?

A. Producer's mill
B. Type of steel and grade of steel
C. Bar size
D. All of the above

Lowering the top bars or raising the bottom bars by 1/2" more than specified in a 6" concrete slab could reduce its load carrying capacity by _____.

A. Approximately 10%
B. Approximately 20%
C. Approximately 15%
D. Approximately 25%

What is the maximum variation of stirrup location in a floor slab?

A. +/- .5"
B. +/- 1"
C. +/- 1.5"
D. +/- 2"

Which of the following is not a type of rebar splice?

A. Mechanical
B. Bundled
C. Welded
D. Lap

What is the minimum length of lap in a lapped splice for reinforcing bars?

A. 8"
B. 10"
C. 12"
D. 14"

The most effective water stops used to stop the seepage of water are made of _____ .

A. Aluminum
B. Magnesium
C. PVC (Polyvinylchloride)
D. None of the above

The Contractors Guide to Quality Concrete Construction, 4th Ed.
Answers

1.	A	14
2.	B	14
3.	C	15
4.	D	13
5.	D	16
6.	B	19
7.	A	20
8.	C	39
9.	B	19
10.	B	121
11.	D	95
12.	A	105
13.	C	100
14.	A	102
15.	D	102
16.	C	110
17.	D	121
18.	B	122
19.	C	123
20.	B	110
21.	A	14
22.	C	127
23.	A	151
24.	C	122
25.	A	124
26.	A	183
27.	A	183
28.	A	183
29.	B	186	Fig. 11.20
30.	B	178
31.	D	194

32.	B	184
33.	C	188
34.	A	127
35.	A	183
36.	C	196
37.	D	198
38.	C	201
39.	A	176
40.	C	12
41.	B	187
42.	D	191
43.	D	122
44.	C	38
45.	C	149
46.	A	12
47.	C	14
48.	B	16/17
49.	C	17
50.	D	17
51.	B	19
52.	B	19
53.	D	20
54.	A	24
55.	C	127
56.	D	38
57.	C	48
58.	A	61
59.	B	64
60.	C	177
61.	B	64
62.	A	66
63.	D	67
64.	C	70

65.	A	74/75
66.	B	82
67.	C	88
68.	C	91
69.	D	94
70.	D	94
71.	B	100
72.	B	101
73.	B	105
74.	C	105
75.	C	113

The Contractors Guide to Quality Concrete Construction
Questions and Answers

The most common type of cement is Type _____ .

A.   I
B.   II
C.   III
D.   IV

High early strength cement is Type _____ .

A.   II
B.   III
C.   IV
D.   V

Low heat hydration cement is Type _____ .

A.   II
B.   III
C.   IV
D.   V

Test cylinders stored on the job would ideally be stored under what conditions?

A.   Controlled moisture
B.   Controlled temperature
C.   Controlled conditions
D.   All of the above

What is not an example of a pozzolan?

A.   Microsilica
B.   Class C Fly Ash
C.   Class F Fly Ash
D.   Granulated slag

A_____ is used to extend the setting time of concrete.

A.   Accelerator
B.   Retarder
C.   Extending agents
D.   Setting inhibitor

7.   _____ accelerates the setting of concrete but is prohibited in pre-stressed concrete designs.

    A.   Calcium chloride
    B.   Fly ash
    C.   Calcium hypochlorite
    D.   Sodium bicarbonate

8.   For hot-weather concreting, a maximum temperature of _____ F is often specified.

    A.   80
    B.   85
    C.   90
    D.   95

9.   You can increase the slump of concrete 5 to 7 inches by adding a/an _____ .

    A.   Retarder
    B.   Superplasticizer
    C.   Accelerator
    D.   Aggregate

10.   You must discharge truck-mixed concrete before _____ revolutions of the mixer.

    A.   200
    B.   300
    C.   500
    D.   600

11.   What is/are the fiber material(s) in fiber-reinforced concrete?

    A.   Glass
    B.   Steel
    C.   Polypropylene
    D.   All of the above

12.   In _____ splice, the bars are lapped next to each other at a certain length and securely wired together with tie wire.

    A.   Lap
    B.   Welded
    C.   Mechanical
    D.   None of the above

13.   For concrete cast against and permanently exposed to earth, minimum cover for bundled bars is _____
    A.   1 inch
    B.   2 inches
    C.   3 inches
    D.   4 inches

4.   What type of wire is used to tie rebars?

        A.   No. 16 gage black soft-annealed wire
        B.   No. 14 gage soft-annealed wire
        C.   No. 16 gage green annealed wire
        D.   No. 12 gage annealed wire

5.   What type of tie is used to secure heavy mats of rebars to be lifted in place by a crane?

        A.   Type A
        B.   Type B
        C.   Type C
        D.   Type D

6.   What is the maximum distance for placing control joints in a wall?

        A.   18 feet
        B.   20 feet
        C.   24 feet
        D.   25 feet

7.   Contraction joints in floors are designed _____ .

        A.   To control random cracking
        B.   So a crack forms at a pre-selected location
        C.   To provide a deliberately weakened plane
        D.   All of the above

8.   Control joints in slabs on grade are made by cutting into the slab to a depth of _____times the slab thickness on the first cut.

        A.   1/8
        B.   1/4
        C.   1/2
        D.   3/4

9.   In an eight (8") slab, control _____ joints should be placed every feet.

        A.   16
        B.   18
        C.   20
        D.   24

0.   What is an isolation joint?

        A.   A joint made to accommodate movements cause by temperature changes
        B.   A joint used at a point of restraint, including the junction between the elements of a structure
        C.   A joint located where one placement ends and the next one begins
        D.   Both A and B

21. What is the purpose of wire mesh placed in slabs on grade?

    A. To prevent the cracks that will occur between the joints from opening
    B. To control crack widths
    C. Both A and B
    D. None of the above

22. Reinforcing wire in slabs should be placed _____ inche(s) from the top of the slab.

    A. 1
    B. 1.5
    C. 2
    D. 2.5

23. What procedure is used to prevent excessive absorption of water from concrete slabs on grade?

    A. Before concreting, moisten the subgrade
    B. Before, concreting saturate the subgrade
    C. Use of a high-range water reducer
    D. None of the above

24. Running concrete over a rough surface in a concrete buggy could cause segregation of the mix.

    A. True
    B. False

25. When pumping concrete the flow must continuous.

    A. True
    B. False

26. When floating air-entrained concrete the bullfloat should be made of what material?

    I. Aluminum
    II. Magnesium
    III. Zinc

    A. I and II
    B. II and III
    C. I only
    D. II only

27. What is used to embed course aggregate particles into the slab?

    A. Checkrod
    B. Vibratory screed
    C. Power float
    D. Wood Float

8. After non-air-entrained concrete is screeded it should be floated with a _____ .

A. Wood float
B. Aluminum float
C. Magnesium float
D. None of the above

9. When should finish trowelling begin?

A. Just before the water sheen disappears
B. After the water sheen has disappeared
C. Immediately after screeding
D. None of the above

10. When can you start the power floating operation?

A. When the operator's footprints will appear on the surface without indenting the concrete
B. The concrete is just firm enough to support the load
C. Both A and B
D. None of the above

11. The maximum height for dropping concrete without an segregation is _____feet.

A. 12
B. 10
C. 8
D. 4

12. Spreading rocks on the surface of a slab and pressing them into the surface is which technique of creating an exposed aggregate finish?

A. Monolithic technique
B. Seeding technique
C. Exposing Technique
D. None of the above

13. Cold weather concreting procedures are required if the average temperature falls below _____degrees F.

A. 60
B. 50
C. 40
D. 30

14. Cold weather concreting requires a curing temperature of degrees _____ F for at three days.

A. 50
B. 60
C. 70
D. 75

35. A non-skid surface on outdoor slabs is created with a _____ .

   A.   Stiff broom
   B.   Texture trowel
   C.   Soft broom
   D.   None of the above

36. Low humidity and wind are the primary causes of rapidly evaporating surface moisture that causes the surface tension resulting in _____ .

   A.   Shrinkage cracks
   B.   Crazing
   C.   Plastic shrinkage cracks
   D.   Blistering

37. Sealing the surface of the concrete before it is fully compacted causes_____ .

   A.   Shrinkage cracks
   B.   Crazing
   C.   Plastic shrinkage cracks
   D.   Blistering

38. Test cylinders stored on the job site should be protected from drying and maintained at a temperature _____ range.

   A.   50 to 70 F
   B.   55 to 75 F
   C.   60 to 80 F
   D.   65 to 85 F

39. What procedure is used to prevent segregation of concrete components when pouring a slab?

   A.   The concrete should be spread as it is deposited
   B.   Deposit the concrete in a pile and then spread with a vibrator
   C.   Addition of an admixture
   D.   None of the above

40. When performing a slump test, each layer is rodded _____ times.

   A.   10
   B.   15
   C.   25
   D.   50

41. The normal curing time for formed concrete is _____ .

   A.   12 to 48 hours
   B.   12 to 72 hours
   C.   48 to 72 hours
   D.   None of the above

. Excessive bleeding can be caused by _____?

  A.   Insufficient fines in mix
  B.   Excess mix water
  C.   Vapor retarded directly under slab
  D.   All of the above

. Sawcutting joints should be done within _____ hours of concrete placement?

  A.   1 to 2
  B.   2 to 6
  C.   4 to 10
  D.   4 to 12

. The maximum delivery time for ready-mixed concrete is _____ minutes.

  A.   30
  B.   60
  C.   90
  D.   120

. 1 gallon of water added to a cubic yard of concrete will increase slump _____ inch.

  A.   ¼
  B.   ½
  C.   1
  D.   2

. What are concrete cylinder tests used for?

  A.   To estimate concrete strength at a given time
  B.   To determine the workability if the mix
  C.   To see if the mix segregates
  D.   To see how much the concrete expands

. When you need concrete to set quickly, what type of concrete should be used to produce high early strength?

  A.   Type I
  B.   Type II
  C.   Type III
  D.   Type IV

. What chemical reaction takes place when portland cement is hardening?

  A.   Permeability
  B.   Hydration
  C.   Dehydration
  D.   None of the above

49. What is the effect of adding too much water to concrete?

    A. Lower slump, higher strength
    B. Lower slump, lower strength
    C. Higher slump, lower strength
    D. Higher slump, higher strength

50. What is the difference between fine & coarse aggregate?

    A. The coarse stone will not pass through a 1/4" sieve
    B. The coarse stone will not pass through a 1/8" sieve
    C. The coarse stone will not pass through a 1/16" sieve
    D. None of the above

51. What should be added to concrete in cold weather?

    A. Calcium hypochlorite
    B. Calcium chloride
    C. Sodium bicarbonate
    D. Fly ash

52. Which of the following is NOT a reason to use an admixture?

    A. To increase early strength
    B. To increase permeability
    C. To increase ultimate strength
    D. To increase workability

53. What is the not true of air-entrained concrete?

    A. Increased workability
    B. Segregation is reduced
    C. Makes concrete more durable
    D. Reduces bleeding

54. What is the effect of adding too much water to a concrete mix?

    A. Higher slump and lower strength
    B. Higher slump, higher strength
    C. Lower slump, lower strength
    D. Lower slump, higher strength

55. Can fly ash be introduced into a concrete mix specifying a minimum cement content?

    A. No
    B. Yes, if called for by the specifier

The maximum delivery time for ready mix concrete after water has been added to the cement is _____ .

A. 30 minutes or 200 revolutions of the mixer drum
B. 60 minutes or 250 revolutions of the mixer drum
C. 90 minutes or 350 revolutions of the mixer drum
D. 90 minutes or 300 revolutions of the mixer drum

Mat, raft or floating foundations are specified when _____ .

A. Budget does not allow for additional cost
B. When builder is looking for a more economical choice
C. The allowable bearing capacity of the soil is very low to great depths
D. None of the above

What type of forms are used to place concrete by extrusion?

A. Slip-forms
B. Jump forms
C. Stay-in-place forms
D. All of the above

What is the minimal quality plywood that can be used when building concrete forms?

A. A-B
B. B-B
C. A-A
D. A-C

What is the best type of nail to use for nailing bracing and forms when the nails must be removed when the pour is completed?

A. Double headed
B. Duplex nails
C. Both A and B
D. Small-head (PTL)

Which of the following is the most economical wood to use for formwork?

A. Cedar
B. Kiln-dried pine
C. Mahogany
D. Oak

The working load of new ties used in formwork should have a safety factor of _____ .

A. 2:1
B. 2:2
C. 3:1
D. 1:2

63.   The purpose for form liners is to provide _____ on concrete surfaces.

       A.   Designs
       B.   Patterns
       C.   Textures
       D.   All of the above

64.   How much does concrete weigh per cubic foot?

       A.   100 lbs.
       B.   125 lbs.
       C.   150 lbs.
       D.   200 lbs.

65.   What is the best way to reduce lateral pressure on concrete forms when placing concrete?

       A.   Slower placement or rate of pour
       B.   Faster placement or rate of pour
       C.   Distributing concrete as it pours out
       D.   None of the above

66.   When an engineer's specifications for removal of concrete forms is not available, the ACI has
       recommendations for the length of time concrete should remain in the forms when the
       air temperature is above _____.

       A.   45 degrees F
       B.   50 degrees F
       C.   60 degrees F
       D.   65 degrees F

67.   What is the main reason for steel reinforcement in a concrete member?

       A.   To increase compressive strength
       B.   To reduce cracking over time
       C.   To resist tensile forces
       D.   None of the above

68.   Placing drawings show details for fabrication and _____ .

       A.   Formwork
       B.   Placing concrete
       C.   Placing of reinforcing steel
       D.   None of the above

69.   What are the characteristics of a #5 bar?

       A.   .325" diameter .20% area 1.022 lbs. per lineal foot
       B.   .425" diameter .21% area 1.033 lbs. per lineal foot
       C.   .525" diameter .31% area 1.032 lbs. per lineal foot
       D.   .625" diameter .31% area 1.043 lbs. per lineal foot

. What do the markings on rebar represent?

A. Producers mill
B. Type of steel and grade of steel
C. Bar size
D. All of the above

. Lowering the top bars or raising the bottom bars by 1/2" more than specified in a 6" concrete slab could reduce its load carrying capacity by _____.

A. Approximately 10%
B. Approximately 20%
C. Approximately 15%
D. Approximately 25%

. What is the maximum variation of stirrup location in a floor slab?

A. +/- .5"
B. +/- 1"
C. +/- 1.5"
D. +/- 2"

. Which of the following is not a type of rebar splice?

A. Mechanical
B. Bundled
C. Welded
D. Lap

. What is the minimum length of lap in a lapped splice for reinforcing bars?

A. 8"
B. 10"
C. 12"
D. 14"

. The most effective water stops used to stop the seepage of water are made of _____ .

A. Aluminum
B. Magnesium
C. PVC (Polyvinylchloride)
D. None of the above

. To what depth should a control joint be cut into a concrete slab?

A. One-eight the slab thickness
B. One-fourth the slab thickness
C. 10% of the slab thickness
D. up to 60% of the slab thickness

77. Joints in concrete should be sawcut within how many hours?

    A.   Within 2 to 8 hours
    B.   Within 4 to 10 hours
    C.   Within 4 to 12 hours12
    D.   Within 6 to 18 hours12

78. When concrete placement is interrupted, what type of joint must be provided?

    A.   A construction joint
    B.   A warping joint
    C.   An isolation joint
    D.   None of the above

79. What is the sole purpose for installing welded wire mesh in a concrete slab?

    A.   To prevent cracks from opening
    B.   To increase-load carrying capacity
    C.   To add flexural strength
    D.   None of the above

80. What is the proper location of welded wire mesh in a concrete slab?

    A.   1" below the slab surface, in the upper half of the slab
    B.   1.5" below the slab surface, in the upper third of the slab
    C.   2" below the slab surface, in the upper third of the slab
    D.   2" below the slab surface, in the upper half of the slab

81. Most specifications allow only one addition of water as long as you do not exceed what?

    A.   Specified slump
    B.   The water to cement ratio
    C.   Admixture to cement ratio
    D.   20 mixer revolutions

82. What is the best shape of aggregate to use when pumping concrete?

    A.   Rounded
    B.   Angular
    C.   Crushed stone
    D.   None of the above

83. When using a 5" diameter pump line, what is the ideal mix to pump?

    A.   4" slump with air entrainment containing no fly ash
    B.   2" slump with air entrainment containing no fly ash
    C.   3" slump with air entrainment containing some fly ash
    D.   4" slump with air entrainment containing some fly ash

A concrete containing a lightweight aggregate should be presoaked to 70 to 80 % total absorption. If not, it will _____ .

A. Segregate
B. Crack when it dries
C. Make pumping more difficult
D. Lose moisture quickly

When using a vibrator on concrete, it should not be kept in one location more than _____ .

A. 1 minute
B. 10 to 15 seconds
C. 20 to 30 seconds
D. 30 to 45 seconds

What type of concrete finish creates a skid-resistant surface?

A. Broom finish
B. Power floating
C. Hand troweled
D. None of the above

Air-entrained concrete is most vulnerable to what type of problem?

A. Blistering
B. Crazing
C. Shrinkage
D. Plastic shrinkage cracks

What temperature should concrete cylinders be maintained at during the first 48 hours prior to testing concrete?

A. 50-70 degrees
B. 60-80 degrees
C. 65-88 degrees
D. 70-80 degrees

According to *The Contractor's Guide for Quality Concrete Construction*, _____ test is not used for quality control.

A. Nuclear density ASTM C 231
B. Air content ASTM C 231 and C 173
C. Compressive strength ASTM C 31 and C39
D. Slump ASTM C143

_____are strips of material placed across a joint to obstruct water seepage.

A. Water retarders
B. Isolation joints
C. Construction joints
D. Waterstops

91. _____ are concrete test that may be specified in a projects specifications.

A. Compressive strength, slump, air, and temperature
B. Compressive strength, slump, and temperature
C. Compressive strength, slump, and air
D. Compressive strength and slump

92. The most common way to determine concrete consistency is determined by one of the following:

A. ASTM D75
B. Soil compression and density
C. Slump
D. With a sodium hydroxide solution

93. Air-entrained concrete, among other benefits, increases the chance of damage due to freezing and thawing.

A. True
B. False

94. Two methods for testing air content in freshly mixed concrete is, _____ .

A. pressure and temperature
B. temperature and volumetric
C. volume and pressure
D. temperature and slump

95. Compressive strength lab tests use concrete cylinders usually 6" in diameter and 12" high.

A. True
B. False

96. _____from a known quantity of ingredients.

A. batch
B. strength
C. yield
D. mix

97. Concrete test cylinder molds are filled with fresh concrete in layers. Each layer will be "rodded" _____times.

A. 15
B. 20
C. 25
D. 30

. Concrete test cylinders are filled with fresh concrete in _____ equal layers.

A. 1
B. 2
C. 3
D. 4

). The chemical and physical changes that occur when Portland cement cures is known as:

A. leaching
B. hydration
C. lactation
D. absorption

)0. The **basic raw** materials of Portland cement are:

A. limestone, clay or shale
B. calcium, silica, iron
C. alumina, limestone, clay
D. alumina, calcium, shale

)1. Type _____ cement is used in massive concrete structures such as dams for low heat of hydration.

A. I
B. II
C. III
D. IV

)2. The primary benefit of microsilica, a pazzolan, is:

A. it's a binder
B. its durability
C. corrosion protection
D. permeability

3. According to *The Contractor's Guide to Quality Concrete Construction*, many specified cements for projects are_____.

A. color control cement
B. blended cement
C. masonry cement
D. expansive cement

4. Type V Portland cement is a high sulfate resistance cement.

A. True
B. False

105. Fly ash is a by-product of:

A. coal-burning
B. coak-burning
C. charcoal-burning
D. wood-burning

106. A higher water/cementitious ratio in a workable concrete batch will decrease its:

A. strength
B. color set
C. cure time
D. slump rock

107. The _____inch sieve is the dividing point between course and fine grade aggregates.

A. #200
B. 1/8"
C. #4
D. 1/4"

108. According to *The Contractor's Guide to Quality Concrete Construction*, non-porous concrete is best achieved by which of the following?

A. low water-to-cement ratio
B. increased moist curing period
C. non-air-entrained concrete and mortar
D. permeability of the paste

109. Concrete aggregates should contain no_____ material or highly porous particles that would prove harmful to the concrete mix.
A. deleterious
B. organic
C. chemical
D. degrading

110. A high-range water reducer, or super plasticizers _____.

I. Requires less water for higher slump
II. Requires less water for lower slump

A. I only
B. II only
C. Either I or II
D. Neither I nor II

1. Super plasticizers in a concrete batch may reduce the amount of water in a batch by as much as _____%.

    A. 10
    B. 20
    C. 30
    D. 40

2. This additive can increase the set-up time and accelerate early strength development of concrete.

    A. pozzolans
    B. calcium hydrate
    C. calcium chloride
    D. sodium chloride

3. Aggregates of a maximum of_____ inch or less is recommended for high strength concrete.

    A. 1/2
    B. 1
    C. 3/4
    D. 3/8

4. According to The According to *The Contractor's Guide to Quality Concrete Construction*, a mix using the largest allowable size aggregate will be the most economical, although a maximum size of _____inch or less is recommended for high-strength concrete.

    A. 1/4
    B. 3/8
    C. 1/2
    D. 3/4

5. Calcium chloride ushould be used in concrete as _____.

    A. a retarder
    B. an accelerator
    C. a hardener
    D. none of these

6. The addition of a superplasticizer typically turns a 2" slump into a _____inch slump.

    A. 2 - 4
    B. 4 - 6
    C. 7 - 9
    D. 10- 13

117. According to *The Contractor's Guide to Quality Concrete Construction*, microscopic air bubbles from air-entraining agents _____.

    A.   makes the concrete more workable
    B.   allows reduction in water content
    C.   makes a more uniform mix
    D.   all of the above

118. Maximum aggregate size is limited by _____ .

    I. Section dimension
    II. Reinforcement spacing

    A.   I only
    B.   II only
    C.   Both I and II
    D.   Neither I nor II

119. According to *The Contractor's Guide to Quality Concrete Construction*, when a water reducer is used i the mix, the same slump can be retained with about _____% less water.

    A.   6 - 8
    B.   8 - 10
    C.   10- 12
    D.   12 - 14

120. Air entrainment in a concrete mix without adjusting the mix will reduce the strength of the batch.

    A.   True
    B.   False

121. "Standard Specifications for Structural Concrete" is also known as:

    A.   American Concrete Institute Standard 301
    B.   American Concrete Institute Standard 302
    C.   American Concrete Institute Standard 318
    D.   American Concrete Institute Standard 319

122. The American Society for Testing and Materials, ASTM, provides standards and specifications for cement materials, concrete aggregates and admixtures. Specifications for cement is under the jurisdiction of committee:

    A.   C 1
    B.   C 5
    C.   C 7
    D.   C 9

3. When pozzolans are used, the water-to-cementitious material ratio (*w/c*) is computed as a water-cementitious material ratio using which of the following formulas?

    A.   (c + m)/w
    B.   (c + w)/m
    C.   w/(c + m)
    D.   m/(c + w)

4. Determine the water-to-cementitious material ratio (*w/c*) with the following data:

1. 450 pounds of cement
2. 270 pounds of water
3. 125 pounds of flyash

A. .495
B. .479
C. .469
D. .457

5. According to *The Contractor's Guide to Quality Concrete Construction*, concrete exposed to severe conditions should be air entrained within what percentage range in mixes with 3/4" to 1" maximum size aggregate?

    A.   4%
    B.   5% - 8%
    C.   9% - 12%
    D.   15%

6. The purpose of a slump test is to measure:

    A.   uniformity
    B.   consistency
    C.   strength
    D.   durability

7. According to *The Contractor's Guide to Quality Concrete Construction*, after 300 drum revolutions or _____ minutes, structural concrete shall be rejected.

    A.   30
    B.   60
    C.   90
    D.   120

8. For hot weather concreting, a maximum concrete temperature of _____ degrees F is often specified.

    A.   85
    B.   87
    C.   90
    D.   92

129. The most common type of shallow foundations are:

   I. Continuous spread footings for walls
   II. Non-continuous spread footings for walls

   A.   I only
   B.   II only
   C.   both I and II
   D.   neither I nor II

130. A _____type of foundation, utilizing heavily reinforced concrete over the entire area of the building, is used when the allowable bearing capacity of the soil is very low to great depths, making pile foundations uneconomical.

   A.   raft
   B.   mat
   C.   floating
   D.   all of the above

131. According to *The Contractor's Guide to Quality Concrete Construction*, the _____ usually designs the forms for cast-in-place concrete.

   A.   Architect
   B.   Owner
   C.   Engineer
   D.   Concrete Contractor

132. Just prior to placing concrete into the forms, you would:

   A.   check to insure that wall-ties are correctly installed
   B.   install stiffeners
   C.   check to insure that connection hardware is installed correctly
   D.   A and C are correct

133. Concrete should be placed at or near as possible to its final position in its forms.

   A.   True
   B.   False

134. Freshly deposited concrete creates pressure against the forms in much the same manner as:

   A.   gravity
   B.   electrostatic pressure
   C.   hydrostatic pressure
   D.   harmonic wave pressure

35. Generally, new concrete shrinks as it hydrates, approximately _____ inches in 100 feet under field conditions.

    A.   1/2
    B.   3/4
    C.   1
    D.   1 1/4

36. Concrete will expand in rainy conditions and shrink in sunny and dry conditions.

    A.   True
    B.   False

37. Internal stress relief in concrete can be evidenced by:

    A.   spelling
    B.   crazing
    C.   dusting
    D.   cracking

38. An isolation joint permits _____ of various parts of the structure.

    A.   differential movement
    B.   isolation
    C.   contraction
    D.   warping

39. What is the maximum distance for placing control joints in a wall?

    A.   18 feet
    B.   20 feet
    C.   24 feet
    D.   25 feet

40. When concrete placement is interrupted, what type of joint must be provided?

    A.   A construction joint
    B.   A warping joint
    C.   An isolation joint
    D.   None of the above

41. Water stops are used to _____.

    A.   obstruct the flow of water
    B.   increase the flow of water
    C.   reduce the flow of water
    D.   obstruct seepage of water

142. According to *The Contractor's Guide to Quality Concrete Construction*, construction, or control joints in concrete slabs are planned cracks induced by cutting into the slab to a depth of _____ the slab thickness, or a minimum of 1 inch, creating a weakened plane.

    A.   1/4
    B.   1/5
    C.   1/6
    D.   15/16

143. Wherever there is a change in cross-sectional area of a slab, there should be _____.

    A. a joint
    B. a construction joint .
    C. a contraction joint
    D. an isolation joint

144. Columns and bases of columns should be separated from the slab by the use of:

    A.   spray on curing compound
    B.   construction joint
    C.   isolation joint
    D.   expansion joint material

145. The term_____ is often used to describe the use of fibers in a concrete mix.

    A.   secondary reinforcement
    B.   fibrous reinforcement
    C.   structural reinforcement
    D.   primary reinforcement

146. Proportions for a concrete mix should be submitted by the hatch plant to the specifier. The procedure is simplest when there is a record of field performance on the batch. This field performance record should include _____ successive tests within the last 12 months.

    A.   1
    B.   15
    C.   30
    D.   90

147. Almost any natural water that is drinkable and has no pronounced odor or taste can be used for making concrete.

    A.   True
    B.   False

148. A method of measuring the penetration resistance of newly placed and cured concrete is the:

    A.   nuclear probe
    B.   Windsor probe
    C.   MRI
    D.   Blue stone dye test

9. Bucket and crane placement of concrete is a very flexible method of concrete placement on large buildings because of:

    A. the ease with which a crane can maneuver for placement
    B. the capacity of modern day concrete placement buckets
    C. the ranee of horizontal and vertical distances available from one position
    D. none of the above

0. The most common method of starting concrete pumping through a line is to start with approximately one cubic yard of a cement-sand slurry.

    A. True
    B. False

1. Vibratory screeds should have the proper balance of _____ to properly consolidate the concrete.

    I. Frequency
    II. Amplitude

    A. I only
    B. II only
    C. both I and II
    D. neither I nor II

2. A darby or bullfloat is used to:

    I. Fill in low spots/cut of high points
    II. Remove excess bleed water

    A. I only
    B. II only
    C. both I and II
    D. neither I nor II

3. According to *The Contractor's Guide to Quality Concrete Construction*, a properly troweled surface will have all of the following characteristics EXCEPT:

    A. hard
    B. even
    C. dense
    D. wear-resistant

4. According to *The According to The Contractor's Guide to Quality Concrete Construction*, hot weather introduces all of the following problems EXCEPT:

    A. lower strength
    B. longer set up time
    C. rapid drying of the surface
    D. shorter set up time

155. Coarse aggregates are usually in the range of _____ inches.

   A.   1/2 " to 2"
   B.   3/8" to 2"
   C.   3/8" to 1 /2"
   D.   1/2" to 1 1/2"

156. According to *The Contractor's Guide to Quality Concrete Construction*, concrete segregation is caused by which of the following?

   A.   placed at a fairly rapid rate
   B.   excessive water to cement ratio
   C.   not enough water, to much cement
   D.   adding superplasticizers

157. A concrete pad is showing signs of dusting. This defect could be the result of _____ during finishing.

   A.   under troweling the surface
   B.   over troweling the surface
   C.   NOT floating the surface
   D.   poor concrete curing

158. Adequate curing is nearly always a preventative measure against almost every common quality problem

   A.   True
   B.   False

159. According to *The Contractors Guide to Quality Concrete Construction*, sprayed-on membrane provides:

   A.   temporary protection against drying
   B.   prevents discoloration due to uneven drying
   C.   efficiency in curing
   D.   all of the above

160. 1 gallon of water added to a cubic yard of concrete will increase slump _____ inch.

   A.   ¼
   B.   ½
   C.   1
   D.   2

The Contractors Guide to Quality Concrete Construction
Answers

1.	A	17
2.	B	17
3.	C	17
4.	D	16
5.	D	17
6.	B	20
7.	A	20
8.	C	31
9.	B	20
10.	B	24
11.	D	68
12.	A	76
13.	C	73
14.	A	74
15.	D	74
16.	C	80
17.	D	87
18.	B	89
19.	C	90
20.	B	79
21.	C	92
22.	C	92
23.	A	98/99
24.	A	122
25.	A	124
26.	A	126
27.	A	125/126
28.	A	126
29.	B	127 Fig. 10.18
30.	C	126
31.	D	134
32.	B	127
33.	C	129
34.	C	129
35.	A	126
36.	C	135
37.	D	138
38.	C	140
39.	A	123
40.	C	14
41.	B	13
42.	D	143
43.	D	89
44.	B	30
45.	C	98
46.	A	15

47.	C	17
48.	B	18
49.	C	18
50.	A	18
51.	B	20
52.	B	20
53.	C	21
54.	A	24
55.	B	29
56.	D	30
57.	C	36
58.	A	47
59.	B	48
60.	C	48
61.	B	48
62.	A	49
63.	D	50
64.	C	52
65.	A	55
66.	B	58
67.	C	63
68.	C	66
69.	D	66
70.	D	68
71.	B	73
72.	B	74
73.	B	76
74.	C	76
75.	C	83
76.	B	88
77.	C	89
78.	A	90
79.	A	92
80.	C	93
81.	B	121
82.	A	123
83.	D	124
84.	C	124
85.	B	124
86.	A	127
87.	A	138
88.	B	140
89.	A	13
90.	D	83
91.	C	13/14
92.	C	13
93.	B	21
94.	C	14
95.	A	14
96.	C	16
97.	C	15

98.	C	15
99.	B	18
100.	A	17
101.	D	17
102.	C	18
103.	B	16/17
104.	A	17
105.	A	17
106.	A	18
107.	D	18
108.	A	18
109.	B	18
110.	A	20
111.	C	20
112.	C	20
113.	C	19
114.	D	19
115.	B	20
116.	C	20
117.	D	21
118.	C	19
119.	B	20
120.	A	21
121.	A	26
122.	D	26
123.	C	18
124.	D	18
125.	B	30
126.	B	23
127.	B	30
128.	C	31
129.	A	34
130.	C	36
131.	D	51
132.	D	53
133.	A	54
134.	C	54
135.	B	78
136.	A	78
137.	D	78
138.	A	81
139.	C	80
140.	A	90
141.	D	83
142.	A	89
143.	C	80
144.	D	91
145.	A	94
146.	C	95
147.	A	18
148.	B	98

149.	C	123
150.	A	123
151.	C	125
152.	A	126
153.	B	126
154.	B	127
155.	C	18/19
156.	B	133
157.	B	137
158.	A	130
159.	C	132
160.	C	98

Modern Masonry, 9th Edition
Questions and Answers

1. In masonry work, _____ is used to make long horizontal joints.

    A. Sled runner
    B. Joint raker
    C. Line jointer
    D. Line runner

2. Concrete should be compacted or vibrated when layers or lifts are up to a maximum _____ inches thick in reinforced concrete.

    A. 8
    B. 10
    C. 12
    D. 14

3. _____ brick is used in dry conditions and exposed to freezing weather.

    A. Grade SW
    B. Grade MW
    C. Grade NW
    D. Grade FBX

4. Brick that will come in contact with ground water and freezing conditions should be _____.

    A. Grade MW
    B. Grade NW
    C. Grade SW
    D. Type FBA

5. With masonry, _____ inch is the unit of measure used in a modular grid system.

    A. 1
    B. 3
    C. 4
    D. 5

6. _____ is the nominal size of a modular brick.

    A. 2" x 2 1/3" x 8"
    B. 3" x 2 2/3" x 8"
    C. 4" x 2 1/3" x 8"
    D. 4" x 2 2/3" x 8"

7. _____ percent of a brick must be solid for it to be considered solid.

    A. 95
    B. 85
    C. 75
    D. 65

8. _____ is the white powder that forms on a masonry wall after exposure to moisture.

    A. Efflorescence
    B. Chalk dust
    C. Fluoropolymer
    D. Sodium bicarbonate

9. Five stretcher courses of brick with one header course describes a _____ bond.

    A. Running
    B. Flemish
    C. English
    D. Common

10. When laying brick and all the vertical joints align, this is a _____ bond.

    A. Dutch
    B. Stack
    C. Flemish
    D. American

11. Which brick pattern is considered the weakest bond?

    A. English cross bond
    B. Common bond
    C. Stack bond
    D. Running bond

12. What type of mortar joint is recommended in areas exposed to high winds and heavy rains?

    A. Weathered
    B. Concave
    C. Troweled
    D. Raked

13. What type of facing tile is used when a high degree of mechanical perfection is required?

    A. FTX unglazed
    B. FTS unglazed
    C. SCR acoustile
    D. SCR unglazed

14. _____ aggregate is expanded shale or clay, expanded slag, coal cinders, pumice, and scoria.

    A. Normal weight
    B. Dense
    C. Lightweight
    D. Coarse

15. The openings in blocks are called _____.

    A. Cross web
    B. Cells
    C. Face shell
    D. Lintels

16. _____ means the quicklime has been formed into putty by combining it with water.

    A. Plasticity
    B. Repointing
    C. Bleeding
    D. Slacked

17. _____ inch is the standard size of a mortar joint when using standard concrete masonry units.

    A. 1/8
    B. ¼
    C. 3/8
    D. ½

18. What is not an advantage of a two-core block CMU versus a three-core block design?

    A. Reduced heat conductor
    B. Lighter
    C. More space for placing conduit
    D. The shell is narrower at the center web

19. A _____ block is used the same way as the corner block but has a rounded corner.

    A. Double corner
    B. Bullnose
    C. Pier
    D. Stretcher

20. A standard glass block mortar joint is _____ inch thick.

    A. 1/8
    B. ¼
    C. ½
    D. 1/3

21. To prevent moisture from entering the top of a masonry wall, you should use _____ copings.

    A. Ceramic tile
    B. Plaster
    C. Wood
    D. Stone

22. What is the best stone to protect against moisture on sills?

    A. Limestone
    B. Granite
    C. Sandstone
    D. Slate

23. Mortar is mainly composed of which cementitious material?

    A. Blended cement
    B. Portland cement
    C. Hydrated lime – Type S
    D. Ground limestone

24. What type of lime is used in mortar?

    A. Type N hydrated
    B. Type M hydrated
    C. Type S hydrated
    D. Type K hydrated

25. What is the primary aggregate used in mortar?

    A. Sand
    B. Quartz
    C. Crushed oyster shells
    D. Gravel

26. To avoid hardening due to hydration, mortar should be used _____ hour(s) after mixing.

    A. 1
    B. 1 ½
    C. 2
    D. 2 ½

27. What type of mortar is best suited for use below grade?

    A. Type S
    B. Type N
    C. Type M
    D. Type O

28. What is the most important property of hardened mortar?

    A. Compressive strength
    B. Bond strength
    C. Durability
    D. Weatherability

29. Which of the following is not a masonry mortar?

    A. Type P
    B. Type O
    C. Type K
    D. Type N

30. What is added to mortar to increase strength?

    A. Admixture
    B. Cement
    C. Aggregate
    D. Polymer

31. What type of mortar is used where wind speeds will exceed 80 miles per hour?

    A. Type K
    B. Type O
    C. Type M
    D. Type N

32. What type of mortar is used for interior non-load bearing partitions where high strength is not needed?

    A. Type S
    B. Type M
    C. Type N
    D. Type K

33. A 10ft x 100ft single wythe brick wall is to be constructed and will have 655 non modular brick per 100 sq ft and 3/8-inch mortar joints. _____ cubic feet of mortar will need to be purchased.

    A. 32
    B. 34
    C. 50
    D. 58

34. _____ are strips of metal or metal wire used to tie masonry wythes together or to tie masonry veneer to a concrete frame or wood frame wall.

   A. Wall ties
   B. Anchors
   C. Joints
   D. Jambs

35. The maximum height of grout lifts is _____ feet.

   A. 3
   B. 5
   C. 7
   D. 9

36. With masonry, what gage wire is ordinarily used for continuous horizontal joint reinforcement?

   A. 5, 6, 7 & 8
   B. 6, 7, 8 & 9
   C. 7, 8, 9 & 10
   D. 8, 9, 10 & 11

37. The closest an adjustable truss type brick tie should be from the edge of the brick is _____ inch.

   A. 3/8
   B. ¾
   C. 5/8
   D. ½

38. When bearing walls intersect, they may be connected with a _____.

   A. Strap anchor
   B. "L" bent bar anchor
   C. Hex coupling
   D. Acorn nut

39. When the cut edge will be hidden by the mortar, which hand tool is used to cut brick?

   A. Masonry saw
   B. Brick hammer
   C. Brick trowel
   D. Brick set chisel

40. When laying brick, what area of the building contains the leads?

   A. The foundation
   B. The first course
   C. The corners
   D. None of the above

41. Wall ties in a brick masonry cavity wall should be placed _____ inch from either edge of the masonry unit.

    A. 3/16
    B. 3/8
    C. 5/8
    D. ½

42. _____ the joint helps the mortar and masonry unit bond together and provide the best moisture protection.

    A. Weathering
    B. Toweling
    C. Raking
    D. Tooling

43. The recommended air pressure setting when using abrasive blasting to clean brick is _____ psf.

    A. 50 – 100
    B. 80 – 120
    C. 60 – 100
    D. 75 – 150

44. When blocks are laid, they are positioned _____.

    A. Narrow flange on top
    B. Wide flange on bottom
    C. Wide flange on top
    D. Narrow flange on bottom

45. _____ is the best cleaning chemical for brick.

    A. Hydrochloric acid
    B. Sulfuric acid
    C. Diluted bleach
    D. Diluted ammonia

46. A two-wythe wall allowing each wythe to react independently to stress known as a _____ wall.

    A. Solid masonry
    B. Cavity
    C. Composite
    D. Reinforced concrete masonry

47. When using 9 gage ties in a composite wall, what is the proper separation of ties?

    A. One for every 4 1/4 square feet
    B. One for every 2 1/2 square feet
    C. One for every 4 1/2 square feet
    D. One for every 2 2/3 square feet

48. When constructing a cavity wall, each wythe is separated by a continuous air space that is at least _____ inch(es) wide.

    A. 1
    B. 1 ½
    C. 2
    D. 2 ½

49. _____ units are masonry units that have been designed for aesthetic appeal.

    A. Ground face
    B. Architectural concrete masonry
    C. Prefaced concrete masonry
    D. Split face masonry

50. What is used to anchor brick veneer to the structure?

    A. Corrugated metal ties
    B. Strap anchors
    C. Flat head anchor
    D. Veneer nails

51. When laying an 8 inches concrete block wall, string out the blocks for the first course without mortar to check layout. Allow for _____ inch each mortar joint.

    A. ¼
    B. ½
    C. 3/8
    D. 5/8

52. The lead corner is usually laid up _____ courses high.

    A. Two to three
    B. Three to four
    C. Four or five
    D. Five to six

53. A _____ inch diameter bar is used to make a 3/8 inch concave mortar joint.

    A. 1/8
    B. 3/8
    C. 5/8
    D. 1/4

54. What type of footings are used for free standing columns or piers?

    A. Stepped
    B. Isolated
    C. Combined
    D. Continuous

55. Foundation walls that are being dampproofed should be parged _____ inches above the finish grade.

    A. 6
    B. 5
    C. 8
    D. 10

56. Masonry exterior non-load bearing walls not supported at each story are known as _____ wall.

    A. Panel
    B. Cavity
    C. Curtain
    D. Solid masonry

57. If the outer wythe of a cavity wall on each side of an external corner extends more than _____ feet, expansion joints are recommended.

    A. 30
    B. 50
    C. 60
    D. 65

58. _____ units are widely used as facing veneer. The veneer is attached to backing but does not act structurally with the rest of the wall.

    A. Brick and stone
    B. Brick and mortar
    C. Stone and concrete
    D. Concrete and glass

59. _____ are placed over an opening in a wall used to support the loads above that opening?

    A. Chases
    B. Recesses
    C. Lintels
    D. Stirrups

60. Welded wire reinforcement for masonry should be lapped to what minimum distance?

    A. One full stay plus 1 inch
    B. Two full stay plus 1 inch
    C. One full stay plus 2 inches
    D. Two full stay plus 2 inches

61. Terrazzo toppings are typically _____ inch thick.

    A. ¼
    B. ½
    C. 3/8
    D. ¾

62. Filling voids in masonry with fresh mortar is known as _____.

    A. Tuckpointing
    B. Joint tucking
    C. Re-grouting
    D. Joint pointing

63. What type of float is used to float large flat slabs?

    A. Hand float
    B. Bull float
    C. Power float
    D. None of the above

64. Open, unsupported stacks of brick should not exceed _____ feet in height.

    A. 5
    B. 6
    C. 7
    D. 8

65. To use a ladder safely be sure it extends at least _____ feet above the point where you plan to step off.

    A. 2
    B. 2.5
    C. 3
    D. 3.5

66. If a plan is drawn 1/4" = 1'0" scale, how long on the drawing would a 40-foot wall be?

    A. 5 inches
    B. 10 inches
    C. 15 inches
    D. 20 inches

67. If a plan is drawn to 1/4 inch size, how long on the drawing would a 40-foot wall be?

    A. 10 feet
    B. 20 feet
    C. 20 inches
    D. 10 inches

68. A hollow masonry unit is one whose cross-sectional area in any plane is less than _____% solid material.

    A. 85
    B. 80
    C. 75
    D. 70

69. The _____ are the tops and bottoms of the bricks or blocks.

    A. Bearing surfaces
    B. Splits
    C. Openings
    D. Bats

70. The simplest mortar joint to make is the _____ joint.

    A. Flush
    B. Rough cut
    C. Raked
    D. Both A and B

71. Hollow load bearing block, ASTM C90, Grade N will have an average minimum compressive strength of _____ psi (individual unit).

    A. 600
    B. 800
    C. 900
    D. 1000

72. An 8" x 8" x 16" block has actual dimensions of _____.

    A. 7 5/8" x 7 5/8" x 15 5/8"
    B. 7 5/8" x 7 3/8" x 15 7/8"
    C. 7 3/8" x 7 3/8" x 15 3/8"
    D. 7 15/16" x 7 15/16" x 15 15/16"

73. Stone is divided into three categories. They are all of the following EXCEPT _____.

    A. Metamorphic
    B. Quartzite
    C. Igneous
    D. Sedimentary

74. Mortar can be retempered by adding water but must be used within _____ hour(s) after original mixing.

    A. 1
    B. 1 ½
    C. 2
    D. 2 ½

75. What ASTM type mortar is used for general use in above ground exposed masonry?

    A. Type N
    B. Type O
    C. Type S
    D. Type M

Please see Answer Key on the following page
3/15/23

Modern Masonry, 9th Edition
Questions and Answers
Answer Key

Answer	Page #	Index
A	27	*Jointers*
C	431	*Concrete – placing and finishing*
B	116	*Brick – classification*
C	116	*Brick – classification*
C	119	*Brick – sizes*
D	120	*Brick – sizes*
	Figure 7-14	
C	123	*Brick – weight*
A	124	*Efflorescence*
D	129	*Pattern bond*
B	130	*Stack bond*
C	130	*Stack bond*
B	131 – 132	*Concave joints*
A	137	*Unglazed facing tile*
C	154	*Lightweight aggregate*
B	160	*Concrete block – block terminology*
D	187	*Hydrate lime*
C	157	*Concrete block – sizes and shapes*
D	157	*Concrete block – sizes and shapes*
B	157	*Concrete block – uses*
B	170	*Glass block*
D	181	*Stone - applications*
A	181	*Stone - applications*
B	187	*Mortar – cementitious materials*
C	187	*Mortar – cementitious materials*
A	188	*Sand*
D	191	*Mortar – hardened*
C	191	*Type M mortar*
B	191	*Mortar – properties*
A	191 – 193	*Mortar – proportions and uses*

Q	Answer	Page #	Index
30.	B	191	*Mortar – properties*
31.	C	191 – 192	*Type M mortar*
		Figure 10-8	
32.	D	193	*Type K mortar*
33.	D	197 - 198	*Mortar – estimating quantities*
		Figure 10-11	

Choose the row with 655 per 100 square ft and would require 5.8 cuft per 100 sq ft of mortar

5.8 cuft / 100 square ft x (10 ft x 100 ft) = 58 cubic feet

Q	Answer	Page #	Index
34.	A	204	*Wall ties*
35.	B	199	*Grout – placement*
36.	D	206	*Metal ties*
37.	C	209	*Adjustable ties*
		Figure 11-11	
38.	A	212	*Anchors*
39.	B	223	*Brick – cutting*
40.	C	230	*Brick walls – laying common*
41.	C	244	*Brick walls – tie place/joint replacement*
42.	D	244	*Brick walls - tooling*
43.	C	254	*Abrasive blasting*
44.	C	266	*Block – handling*
45.	A	252	*Brick – cleaning*
46.	B	260	*Cavity wall*
47.	D	261	*Composite wall*
48.	C	260	*Cavity wall*
49.	B	161	*Concrete block – decorative block*
50.	A	261	*Veneered walls*
51.	C	268	*Block – laying concrete block walls*
52.	C	270	*Block – laying concrete block walls*
		Step #7	
53.	C	272	*Block – laying concrete block walls*
		Step #11	
54.	B	312	*Isolated footing*
55.	A	316	*Dampproofing*

Plan scale is ¼" = 1 ft

¼ = .25" = 1 ft

.25"/1 ft = x / 40ft

X = 40 (.25")

X = 10 inches

40 ft x ¼ = 10 ft

Modern Masonry, 8th Ed.
Questions and Answers

1. In masonry work, what tool is used to make long horizontal joints?

    A.   Sled runner jointer
    B.   Joint raker
    C.   Line jointer
    D.   Line runner

2. Concrete should be compacted or vibrated when layers or lifts are up to a maximum____ inches thick in reinforced concrete.

    A.   8 inches
    B.   10 inches
    C.   12 inches
    D.   14 inches

3. What type of brick is used in dry conditions and exposed to freezing weather?

    A.   SW
    B.   MW
    C.   NW
    D.   FBX

4. Brick that will come in contact with ground water and freezing conditions should be type_____.

    A.   MW
    B.   NW
    C.   SW
    D.   FBA

With masonry, what unit of measure is used in a modular grid system?

    A.   1"
    B.   3"
    C.   4"
    D.   5"

What is the nominal size of a modular brick?

    A.   2" x 2 1/3" x 8"
    B.   3" x 2 2/3" x 8"
    C.   4" x 2 1/3" x 8"
    D.   4" x 2 2/3" x 8"

What percentage of a brick must be solid for it to be considered solid?

    A.   95%
    B.   85%
    C.   75%
    D.   65%

What is the white powder that forms on a masonry wall after exposure to moisture?

    A.   Efflorescence
    B.   Chalk dust
    C.   Fluoropolymer
    D.   Sodium bicarbonate

Five stretcher courses of brick with one header course describe what type of bond?

    A.   Running
    B.   Flemish
    C.   English
    D.   Common

. When laying brick and all the vertical joints align, this is a_____.

    A.   Dutch bond
    B.   Stack bond
    C.   Flemish bond
    D.   American bond

11. Which brick pattern is considered the weakest bond?

    A.   English cross bond
    B.   Common bond
    C.   Stack bond
    D.   Running bond

12. What type of mortar joint is recommended in areas exposed to high winds and heavy rains?

    A.   Weathered joint
    B.   Concave
    C.   Troweled joint
    D.   Raked joint

13. What type of facing tile is used when a high degree of mechanical perfection is required?

    A.   FTX unglazed
    B.   FTS unglazed
    C.   SCR acoustile
    D.   SCR unglazed

14. What is the weight of an 8 x 8 x 16 CMU made of sand & gravel?

    A.   28 lbs.
    B.   35 lbs.
    C.   40 lbs.
    D.   42 lbs.

15. What is the highest strength aggregate in an 8 x 8 x 16 CMU?

    A.   Shale
    B.   Sand and gravel
    C.   Expanded slag
    D.   Scoria

16. Which CMU weighs the least per cubic foot of concrete?

    A.   Sand
    B.   Limestone
    C.   Air-cooled slag
    D.   Pumice

. What is the standard size of a mortar joint when using standard concrete masonry units?

    A.   1/8"
    B.   ¼"
    C.   3/8"
    D.   ½"

. What is not an advantage of a two-core block CMU versus a three-core block design?

    A.   Reduced heat conductor
    B.   Lighter
    C.   More space for placing conduit
    D.   The shell is narrower at the center web

. The nominal size of an 8-inch stretcher block is_____.

    A.   6 x 6 x 18
    B.   8 x 8 x 16
    C.   8 x 8 x 12
    D.   10 x 10 x 18

. A standard glass block mortar joint is how thick?

    A.   1/8 inch
    B.   ¼ inch
    C.   ½ inch
    D.   1/3 inch

. To prevent moisture from entering the top of a masonry wall, you should use_____.

    A.   Ceramic tile copings
    B.   Plaster copings
    C.   Wood copings
    D.   Stone copings

. What is the best stone to protect against moisture on sills?

    A.   Limestone
    B.   Granite
    C.   Sandstone
    D.   Slate

23. Mortar is mainly composed of which cementitious material?

    A.   Blended cement
    B.   Portland cement
    C.   Hydrated lime – Type S
    D.   Ground limestone

24. What type of lime is used in mortar?

    A.   Type N hydrated
    B.   Type M hydrated
    C.   Type S hydrated
    D.   Type K hydrated

25. What is the primary aggregate used in mortar?

    A.   Sand
    B.   Quartz
    C.   Crushed oyster shells
    D.   Gravel

26. To avoid hardening due to hydration, mortar should be used within what time span after mixing?

    A.   1 hour
    B.   1 ½ hours
    C.   2 hours
    D.   2 ½ hours

27. What type of mortar is best suited for use below grade?

    A.   Type S
    B.   Type N
    C.   Type M
    D.   Type O

28. What is the most important property of hardened mortar?

    A.   Compressive strength
    B.   Bond strength
    C.   Durability
    D.   Weather ability

. Which of the following is not a masonry mortar?

    A.   Type P
    B.   Type O
    C.   Type K
    D.   Type N

. What is added to mortar to increase strength?

    A.   Admixture
    B.   Cement
    C.   Aggregate
    D.   Polymer

. What type of mortar is used where wind speeds will exceed 80 miles per hour?

    A.   Type K
    B.   Type O
    C.   Type S
    D.   Type N

. What type of mortar is used for interior non-load bearing partitions where high strength is not needed?

    A.   Type S
    B.   Type M
    C.   Type N
    D.   Type K

. How many cubic feet of mortar are required for a single wythe brick wall that measures 200 square feet, s 3/8" mortar joints and has 655 non-modular brick units per 100 square feet?

    A.   6.8 cubic feet
    B.   11.6 cubic feet
    C.   12.8 cubic feet
    D.   14.4 cubic feet

34. Per 100 sq ft, using a 3/8" mortar joint, you will need how many brick and how many cubic feet of mortar?

    A.   655 brick and 5.8 cubic feet of mortar
    B.   616 brick and 7.2 cubic feet of mortar
    C.   470 brick and 5.8 cubic feet of mortar
    D.   432 brick and 4.5 cubic feet of mortar

35. The maximum height of grout lifts is usually how high?

    A.   3 feet
    B.   5 feet
    C.   7 feet
    D.   9 feet

36. With masonry, what gauge wire is ordinarily used for continuous horizontal joint reinforcement?

    A.   5, 6, 7 & 8
    B.   6, 7, 8 & 9
    C.   7, 8, 9 & 10
    D.   8, 9, 10 & 11

37. What is the closest an adjustable truss type brick tie should be from the edge of the brick?

    A.   3/8"
    B.   ¾"
    C.   5/8"
    D.   ½"

38. When masonry walls intersect, they may be connected with a?

    A.   Strap anchor
    B.   "L" bent bar anchor
    C.   Hex coupling
    D.   Acorn nut

39. When the cut edge will be hidden by the mortar, which hand tool is used to cut brick?

    A.   Masonry saw
    B.   Brick hammer
    C.   Brick trowel
    D.   Brick set chisel

. When laying brick, what area of the building contains the leads?

    A.   The foundation
    B.   The first course
    C.   The corners
    D.   None of the above

. Wall ties in a brick masonry cavity wall should be placed what distance from either edge of the masonry unit?

    A.   3/16"
    B.   3/8"
    C.   5/8"
    D.   ½"

. Which masonry joint provides the best moisture protection?

    A.   Weathered joint
    B.   Toweled joint
    C.   Raked joint
    D.   Tooled joint

. What is the recommended air pressure setting when sandblasting brick with a ¼" nozzle?

    A.   50 – 100 psf
    B.   80 – 120 psf
    C.   60 – 100 psf
    D.   75 – 150 psf

. When blocks are laid, they are positioned how?

    A.   Narrow flange on top
    B.   Wide flange on bottom
    C.   Wide flange on top
    D.   Narrow flange on bottom

. What is the best cleaning chemical for brick?

    A.   Hydrochloric or muratic acid
    B.   Sulfuric acid
    C.   Diluted bleach
    D.   Diluted ammonia

46. What is a two-wythe wall allowing each wythe to react independently to stress known as?

    A.   Solid masonry wall
    B.   Cavity wall
    C.   Composite wall
    D.   Reinforced concrete masonry wall

47. When using 9 gage ties in a composite wall, what is the proper separation of ties?

    A.   One for every 4 1/4 square feet
    B.   One for every 2 1/2 square feet
    C.   One for every 4 1/2 square feet
    D.   One for every 2 2/3 square feet

48. When constructing a two wythe wall, what is the most common cavity size?

    A.   1"
    B.   1.5"
    C.   2"
    D.   2.5"

49. What type of CMU is commonly used with reinforcement?

    A.   Double bull nose block
    B.   2 core block
    C.   3 core block
    D.   Sash block

50. What is used to anchor brick veneer to the structure?

    A.   Corrugated metal ties
    B.   Strap anchors
    C.   Flat head anchor
    D.   Veneer nails

51. When laying an 8" concrete block wall, string out the blocks for the first course without mortar to che
    layout. Allow for _____ each mortar joint.

    A.   ¼"
    B.   ½"
    C.   3/8"
    D.   5/8"

. The lead corner is usually laid up how many courses high?

    A.   Two to three courses
    B.   Three to four courses
    C.   Four or five courses high
    D.   Five to six courses

. What diameter bar is used to make a 3/8" concave mortar joint?

    A.   1/8 inch
    B.   3/8 inch
    C.   5/8 inch
    D.   1/4 inch

. What type of footings are used for free standing columns or piers?

    A.   Stepped
    B.   Isolated
    C.   Combined
    D.   Continuous

. Foundation walls that are being damp-proofed should be parged how many inches above the finish grade?

    A.   6"
    B.   5"
    C.   8"
    D.   10"

. What are masonry exterior non-load bearing walls not supported at each story?

    A.   Panel wall
    B.   Cavity wall
    C.   Curtain walls
    D.   Solid masonry wall

. How long must the outer wythe of a cavity wall be on each side of an external corner before expansion joints are recommended?

    A.   30 feet
    B.   50 feet
    C.   60 feet
    D.   65 feet

58. A brick veneer wall will not support loads.

    A.   True
    B.   False

59. What masonry structural member is placed over an opening in a wall used to support the loads above that opening?

    A.   Chases
    B.   Recesses
    C.   Lintel
    D.   Stirrups

60. Welded wire mesh for masonry should be lapped to what minimum distance?

    A.   One full wire grid spacing plus 1 inch
    B.   Two full wire grid spacing plus 1 inch
    C.   One full wire grid spacing plus 2 inches
    D.   Two full wire grid spacing plus 2 inches

61. How thick are terrazzo toppings typically?

    A.   ¼"
    B.   ½"
    C.   3/8"
    D.   ¾"

62. What is filling voids in masonry with fresh mortar known as?

    A.   Tuck pointing
    B.   Joint tucking
    C.   Re-grouting
    D.   Joint pointing

63. What type of float is used to float large flat slabs?

    A.   Hand float
    B.   Bull float
    C.   Power float
    D.   None of the above

. Open, unsupported stacks of brick should not exceed _____ feet in height.

 A. 5"
 B. 6"
 C. 7"
 D. 8"

. To use a ladder safely be sure it extends at least _____ feet above the point where you plan to step off.

 A. 2"
 B. 2.5"
 C. 3"
 D. 3.5"

. If a plan is drawn 1/4" = scale, how long on the drawing would a 40' wall be?

 A. 10 feet
 B. 10 inches
 C. 4 feet
 D. 4 inches

. If a plan is drawn to 1/4" **size**, how long on the drawing would a 40' wall be?

 A. 10 feet
 B. 10 inches
 C. 4 feet
 D. 4 inches

. A hollow masonry unit is one whose cross-sectional area in any plane is less than _____ % solid material.

 A. 85
 B. 80
 C. 75
 D. 70

The term that describes a white powder or salt like deposit on masonry walls is _____.

 A. Efflorescence
 B. Chalk dust
 C. Fluoropolymer
 D. Sodium bicarbonate

70. The simplest mortar joint to make is the _____ joint.

    A.   Flush
    B.   Rough cut
    C.   Raked
    D.   Both A and B

71. Hollow load bearing block, ASTM C90, Grade N will have an average minimum compressive strength of _____ psi (individual unit).

    A.   600
    B.   800
    C.   900
    D.   1000

72. An 8" x 8" x 16" block has actual dimensions of _____.

    A.   7 5/8" x 7 5/8" x 15 5/8"
    B.   7 5/8" x 7 3/8" x 15 7/8"
    C.   7 3/8" x 7 3/8" x 15 3/8"
    D.   7 15/16" x 7 15/16" x 15 15/16"

73. Stone is divided into three categories. They are all of the following EXCEPT:

    A.   Metamorphic
    B.   Quartzite
    C.   Igneous
    D.   Sedimentary

74. Mortar can be retempered by adding water but must be used within _____ hour(s) after original mixing.

    A.   1 hour
    B.   1.5 hours
    C.   2 hours
    D.   2.5 hours

75. What ASTM type mortar is used for general use in above ground exposed masonry?

    A.   Type N
    B.   Type O
    C.   Type S
    D.   Type M

Please See Answer Key on following page
ALH 11/13/2019

1 Exam Prep
Modern Masonry
Questions and Answers

ANSWER KEY

Answer	**Section/Page#**
1. A	Page 6
2. C	Page 379
3. B	Page 82
4. C	Page 82
5. C	Page 85
6. D	Page 87
7. C	Page 91
8. A	Page 92
9. D	Page 96
10. B	Page 97
11. C	Page 97
12. B	Page 99
13. A	Pages 104
14. C	Page 119
15. B	Page 119
16. D	Page 119
17. C	Page 122
18. D	Page 128
19. B	Page 123
20. B	Page 132
21. D	Page 144
22. A	Page 143
23. B	Page 148
24. C	Page 148
25. A	Page 149
26. D	Page 152

Answer		**Section/Page#**
27. C		Page 152
28. B		Page 152
29. A		Page 153
30. B		Page 153
31. C		Page 154
32. D		Page 154
33. B		Page 159, (refer to figure 8-8, double the amount).
34. A		Page 159
35. B		Page 161
36. D		Page 167
37. C		Page 169
38. A		Page 173
39. B		Page 182
40. C		Page 187
41. C		Page 200
42. D		Page 200
43. C	.	Page 210
44. C		Page 220
45. A		Page 208
46. B		Page 214
47. D		Page 216
48. C		Page 214
49. B		Page 216
50. A		Page 216
51. C		Page 222
52. C		Page 224
53. C		Page 225
54. B		Page 262
55. A		Page 268
56. C		Page 278
57. B		Page 283

BCSI – Guide to Good Practice for Handling, Installing, Restraining and Bracing of Metal Plate Connected Wood Trusses, 2018 (Updated 2020) Questions and Answers

1. For truss spans greater than 60 feet, a spreader bar should be attached to the top chords and web members at intervals of _____ feet.

    A. 12
    B. 10
    C. 8
    D. 5

2. The maximum bow allowed for a truss length of approximately 20 feet is _____ inch(es).

    A. ¼
    B. ½
    C. 2
    D. 1 ¼

3. The spacing of trusses along the bearing support must be within _____ inch(es) of the plan dimensions.

    A. +/- ¼
    B. +/- ½
    C. +/- 1
    D. +/- 1 ½

4. The maximum allowable stack height of plywood or OSB on trusses (assume trusses designed with a live load of 40 psf or greater) is _____ inches.

    A. 16
    B. 12
    C. 10
    D. 8

5. The _____ hand signal is represented by holding both fists in front of the body with thumbs pointing toward each other.

    A. Extend boom
    B. Lower boom
    C. Raise boom
    D. Retract boom

6. If trusses are to be stored horizontally for more than one week, place blocking of sufficient height beneath the stack of trusses at intervals not to exceed _____ feet.

    A. 10
    B. 8
    C. 6
    D. 4

7. Any field modifications that involves the cutting or drilling of truss members must be approved by the _____.

    A. Contractor
    B. Truss manufacturer
    C. Engineer
    D. Architect

8. Top chord bearing flat or parallel chord trusses shall be installed so that the gap between the inside edge of the bearing and the first diagonal or vertical web member does not exceed _____ inch.

    A. 1/8
    B. ¼
    C. ½
    D. ¾

9. It is important to provide substantial bracing for the first truss erected. After the first set of trusses is adequately _____ braced, the remaining trusses installed rely on this first set for stability.

    A. Ground
    B. Diagonally
    C. Restrained and
    D. Temporarily

10. Install web diagonal braces so that they cross the web members at approximately 45 degrees and are nailed with a minimum of _____ nail(s) at each end and at each intersecting Truss web.

    A. 1
    B. 2
    C. 3
    D. 4

11. Trusses with spans less than or equal to _____ feet can be raised into position by lifting near the peak.

    A. 8
    B. 10
    C. 15
    D. 20

12. For 2 x 6 or greater lateral restraint and diagonal bracing, use a minimum of _____ nail(s) per connection.

    A. 1
    B. 2
    C. 3
    D. 4

13. To help transfer large bracing forces onto the roof and ceiling diaphragms, dimension lumber _____ may need to be installed between the trusses.

    A. Blocking
    B. Purlins
    C. Stubs
    D. Girders

14. Use at least _____ nails into each truss for both lateral restraint and diagonal bracing members.

    A. 2 - 16d
    B. 4 - 10d
    C. 1 - 12d
    D. 3 - 16d

15. BCSI is primarily directed toward truss installation in which the on-center (oc) spacing is _____ inch or less.

    A. 10
    B. 12
    C. 24
    D. 36

16. Bottom chord temporary lateral restraint (BCTLR) shall be installed as continuous rows spaced no mor▪ than _____ feet on center.

    A. 10
    B. 12
    C. 15
    D. 18

17. A truss with a depth of _____ feet can only be out of plumb by $1\frac{1}{4}$ inches to be considered to be in compliance with installation tolerances.

    A. 3
    B. 4
    C. 5
    D. 6

18. Attach the lateral restraint at the locations shown on TDD together with a diagonal brace at an angle of less than or equal to _____ degrees to the lateral restraint.

    A. 30
    B. 45
    C. 60
    D. 90

19. Hip jacks and end jacks should be installed a maximum _____ feet on center.

    A. 6
    B. 8
    C. 10
    D. 12

20. The maximum height that concrete block can be stacked on trusses that are properly restrained and braced first is _____ inches.

    A. 4
    B. 6
    C. 8
    D. 10

21. The minimum length of web reinforcement for single-ply trusses is 90% of the web or to extend within _____ inches of end of the web member, whichever is greater.

    A. 4
    B. 6
    C. 8
    D. 10

22. The maximum length of truss that can be picked without the use of a spreader bar is _____ feet.

    A. 20
    B. 30
    C. 40
    D. 50

23. Use a minimum of _____ stress-graded lumber for web diagonal braces.

    A. 2 x 2
    B. 2 x 4
    C. 2 x 6
    D. 2 x 8

24. The maximum top chord temporary lateral restraint spacing for a truss span 30 – 45 feet is _____ feet on center.

    A. 4
    B. 6
    C. 8
    D. 10

25. The maximum on center spacing of a permanent lateral restraint is _____ feet.

    A. 8
    B. 10
    C. 12
    D. 15

26. When lifting trusses over 30 feet long, a _____ must be used.

    A. Spreader bar
    B. Lateral restraint
    C. Slip knot
    D. Chain and hooks

27. When unloading trusses with a crane, the operator should NOT _____.

    A. Store on even blocks
    B. Brace to prevent tipping
    C. Avoid lateral bends
    D. Lift by web member

28. If a wood truss has a depth of 10 feet, the maximum out-of-plumb tolerance is _____ inch.

    A. 2
    B. 1 ¾
    C. 1 ½
    D. 1 ¼

29. Place material _____ when stacking on trusses.

    A. At the peak and next to load bearing wall
    B. Perpendicular to the truss and at the peak
    C. Next to load bearing wall or directly over interior load bearing wall
    D. Directly on top of the chords

30. Use a minimum 2 x 4 stress-graded lumber connected with a minimum _____ nails at each junction for restraint and bracing material.

    A. 2 – 16d
    B. 4 – 10d
    C. 1 – 12d
    D. 3 – 16d

31. Contractor experience is required to install trusses _____ feet and greater in span.

    A. 12
    B. 24
    C. 30
    D. 60

32. A maximum _____ pounds load can be placed on unbraced trusses.

    A. 100
    B. 200
    C. 500
    D. None of the above

33. A 25-foot truss should not be installed if it has an overall bow that is greater than _____ inch.

    A. 1
    B. 1 ¼
    C. 1 ½
    D. 1 ¾

34. Wood moisture content exceeding _____ percent must be taken in account when developing the design of the trusses for a building.

    A. 5
    B. 10
    C. 15
    D. 19

35. An (a) _____ used to hoist a truss shall be of sufficient strength and rigidity to carry the weigh and to resist the bending of the truss.

    A. Outrigger
    B. Crane
    C. Spreader bar
    D. Hoist

36. Use at least _____ lift points for bundles with top chord pitch trusses greater than 60 feet and parallel chord trusses greater than 45 feet.

    A. 1
    B. 2
    C. 3
    D. 4

37. _____ ground bracing ties the first set of trusses off to a series of braces that are attached to stak driven in the ground.

   A. Lateral
   B. Diagonal
   C. Exterior
   D. Interior

38. _____ plane requires temporary/permanent diagonal bracing.

   A. Top chord
   B. Bottom chord
   C. Parallel chord
   D. Web member

39. _____ is/are the horizontal distance(s) between outside edges of exterior bearings.

   A. Panel points
   B. Continuous lateral span
   C. Truss spacings
   D. Truss span

40. _____ are trusses specially designed to carry extra loads from framing and equipment.

   A. Girders
   B. Mono trusses
   C. Scissor trusses
   D. Parallel chord trusses

41. The nails for toe-nailing jack truss to girder connections are assumed to be installed at _____ inc from the end of the jack truss.

   A. 1 1/8
   B. 1 ¼
   C. 1 ½
   D. 1 ¾

42. Truss heel height is the _____.

   A. Vertical length of the truss at the outside face of bearing
   B. Vertical length of the truss at the inside face of bearing
   C. Vertical depth of the truss at the outside face of bearing
   D. Vertical depth of the truss at the inside face of bearing

43. Diagonal bracing should be run at to at least the fourth truss on _____ feet and wider buildings.

   A. 24
   B. 36
   C. 44
   D. 48

44. Each employee engaged in residential construction activities _____ feet or more above lower levels shall be protected by guardrail systems, scaffolding, a safety net system or a personal fall arrest system.

    A. 4
    B. 6
    C. 8
    D. 10

Please see Answer Key on the following page

BCSI – Guide to Good Practice for Handling, Installing, Restraining and Bracing of Metal Plate Connected Wood Trusses, 2018 (Updated 2020)
Questions and Answers
Answer Key

	Answer	**Page#**	
1.	B	9	Figure B1-12A
2.	D	11	Table B1-3 Out of Plane
3.	A	11	
4.	A	53	Table B4-1 Maximum Stack Height for Material on Trusses
5.	D	5	
6.	A	4, 75	
7.	B	16	
8.	C	11	
9.	B	10	
10.	B	26	
11.	D	9	
12.	C	81	
13.	A	42	
14.	A	10	
15.	C	viii	
16.	C	27	
17.	C	11	Table B1-2 Out of Plumb
18.	B	41	
19.	C	30	
20.	C	53	
21.	B	45	
22.	B	8	
23.	B	26	
24.	C	12	Table B1-4 Maximum Top Chord Temporary Lateral Restraint Spacing
25.	B	13	
26.	A	9	Figure B1-10B
27.	D	6	
28.	A	11	
29.	C	15	
30.	A	19	
31.	D	33	
32.	D	53	
33.	C	11	
34.	D	xi	
35.	C	6	
36.	C	7	

	Answer	Page#
.	C	10
.	D	12
.	D	98
.	A	69
.	A	66
.	C	98
.	D	79
.	B	89

1 Exam Prep
BCSI – Guide to Good Practice for Handling, Installing, 2013
Restraining and Bracing of Metal Plate Connected Wood Trusses
Questions and Answers - 1

1. For truss spans greater than 60', a strong-back should be attached to the top cord and web members at intervals of approximately _____.

    A. 12 feet
    B. 10 feet
    C. 8 feet
    D. 5 feet

2. The approximate out-of-plane tolerance for a 20'long truss is _____.

    A. ¼"
    B. 1/2:"
    C. 2"
    D. 1-1/4"

3. The spacing of trusses along the bearing support should be within _____ of the plan dimensions.

    A. +/- ¼"
    B. +/- ½"
    C. +/- 1"
    D. 0"

4. What is the maximum allowable stack height of plywood or OSB on trusses (assume trusses designed with a live load of 40 psf or greater).

    A. 16 feet
    B. 12 feet
    C. 10 feet
    D. 8 feet

5. Which of the following is not correct?

    A. Do not lift bundled trusses by their strapping
    B. Walking on trusses that are lying flat should be strictly prohibited
    C. Storing of trusses in a vertical position should be strictly prohibited
    D. No construction loads of any description should be placed on unbalance trusses

For jobsite storage wood trusses must be supported at intervals not exceeding _____ feet.

    A. 10
    B. 8
    C. 6
    D. 4

Cutting or drilling of truss members in the field must be approved by the _____ .

    A. Contractor
    B. Owner.
    C. Engineer
    D. Architect

According to BCSI, top chord bearing parallel chord trusses should have a maximum gap between the inside bearing and the first diagonal of vertical web of _____ .

    A. 0.0"
    B. ½"
    C. 1/4"
    D. 0.75"

Chord trusses may buckle or collapse if they do not have temporary lateral bracing and temporary _____ .

    A. pulling connections
    B. diagonal bracing
    C. ground bracing
    D. purlins

What span length of truss can be safely lifted without the use of a spreader?

    A. 20' and longer
    B. 30' or less
    C. 40' or less
    D. 35' or less

What is the recommended size and length of the lumber to be used for temporary bracing for truss erection?

    A. 1 x 4, by 8'
    B. a x 6, by 10'
    C. 2 x 4, by 10'
    D. 1 x 4, by 12'

12. Given: Top Chord Size: 2 x 10
            Grade: No. 1 Southern Pine
            Maximum spacing between rows of lateral restraint: 8 feet

What is the maximum truss span that can be safely restrained?

    A. 40 feet
    B. 35 feet
    C. 30 feet
    D. 25 feet

13. The maximum gap between the inside of the first diagonal bearing and the bearing wall of a top chord bearing flat or parallel chord truss is _____.

    A. 0"
    B. ¼"
    C. ½"
    D. 1"

14. For web diagonal braces, used for wood trusses, they must be installed so that they cross at about 45° and are nailed at a minimum of _____.

    A. 2 each 16d nails
    B. 4 each 10d nails
    C. 1 each 12d nails
    D. 3 each 16d nails

15. A contractor is going to set a 70' long wood truss. According to BCSI, it must be picked with a strongback attached to the top chord and web members at intervals of approximately _____.

    A. 6 feet
    B. 8 feet
    C. 10 feet
    D. 12 feet

16. According to BCSI, when setting 40' trusses with a 5/12 slope the bottom chord must have temporary bracing spaced at a maximum of _____.

    A. 10'
    B. 12'
    C. 15'
    D. 18'

The maximum bow for a truss length of 25 feet is _____.

    A. 7/8"
    B. ¾"
    C. 1"
    D. 1-1/2"

Any correction, which involves the cutting or drilling of truss members in the field must be approved by _____.

    A. Contractor
    B. Architect
    C. Engineer
    D. Owner

Temporary lateral bracing is not sufficient to prevent the collapse of group trusses; it should always be used conjunction with _____ braces.

    A. ground
    B. bottom chord
    C. lapped
    D. diagonal

The top chord lateral bracing would be spaced at _____ feet for a 40' truss at a slope of 4/12.

    A. 4'
    B. 6'
    C. 8'
    D. 10'

For a 40' span scissor truss with 5/12 slope and a pitch difference of 3, would require top chord lateral cing spaced at _____ .

    A. 4'
    B. 6'
    C. 8'
    D. 10'

What is the maximum length of truss that can be picked without the use of a spreader bar?

    A. 20'
    B.. 30'
    C. 40'
    D. 50'

23. When installing 2 x 4 diagonal bracing _____ nails are used.

      A. 2 – 8d
      B. 2 – 12d
      C. 2 – 16 d
      D. None of the above

24. The maximum top chord temporary lateral restrain spacing for a truss span 30-45 feet is _____.

      A. 4 feet on center
      B. 6 feet on center
      C. 8 feet on center
      D. 10 feet on center

25. With lateral bracing at least _____ trusses should be lapped.

      A. 1
      B. 2
      C. 3
      D. 4

1 Exam Prep
BCSI – Guide to Good Practice for Handling, Installing, 2013 Restraining and Bracing of Metal Plate Connected Wood Trusses
Questions and Answers - 1

B	Page 8, Page 9 Figure B1-12A and B1-12B
D	Page 11, Table B1-3
A	Page 11
A	Page 53, Table B4-1
C	Page 3
A	Page 3 and Page 75, Bio-3
C	Page 16
B	Page 59, Figure B7-3
B	Page 10
B	Page 8
C	Page 9, Figure B1-16
A	Page 79, Table B10-1
C	Page 11
A	Page 9, Table B1-1
C	Page 9, Figure B1-12B
C	Page 27, Figure B2-35
D	Page 11, Table B1-3
C	Page 55
D	Page 10
C	Page 12, Table B1-4
C	Page 12, Table B1-4
B	Page 8
C	Page 9, Table B1-1
C	Page 12, Table B1-4
B	Page 13, FigureB1-28

1 Exam Prep
BCSI – Guide to Good Practice for Handling, Installing, Restraining and Bracing of Metal Plate Connected Wood Trusses
Questions and Answers - 2

1. When lifting trusses over 30 feet long a _____ must be used.

    A. spreader bar
    B. lateral restraint
    C. slip knot
    D. chain and hooks

2. When unloading trusses with a crane, the operator should NOT _____ .

    A. store on even blocks
    B. brace to prevent tipping
    C. avoid lateral bends
    D. lift by web member

3. The minimum size lumber used as Lateral Restraint and Diagonal Bracing for wood trusses is _____.

    A. 2 x 6
    B. 2 x 4
    C. 1 x 4
    D. All of the above

4. If a wood truss has a rise of 6', the maximum out-of-plumb tolerance is _____ .

    A. 2"
    B. 1 ½"
    C. 3"
    D. 6"

5. A 25 foot truss should not be installed if it has an overall bow that is greater than _____.

    A. 1"
    B. 1 ¼"
    C. 1 ½"
    D. 1 ¾"

_____is the proper placement of plywood when stacking on trusses?

    A. at the peak and next to load bearing wall
    B. perpendicular to the truss and at the peak
    C. next to load bearing wall and perpendicular to the truss
    D. None of the above

Using _____nails at each nailing point is the proper way to nail diagonal web bracing.

    A. 2 – 16d
    B. 4 – 10d
    C. 1 – 12d
    D. 3 – 16d

_____is the maximum allowable spacing for diagonal bracing along top chords.

    A. 20'
    B. 15'
    C. 12'
    D. 8'

How much load can be placed on unbraced trusses?

    A. 100 lbs
    B. 200 lbs
    C. 500 lbs
    D. None of the above

. If jobsite modification of a truss is needed _____.

    A. Modify the truss
    B. Never modify the truss
    C. Consult the designer/engineer
    D. Consult the owner

_____is the maximum allowable spacing for diagonal bracing along bottom chords?

    A. 8'
    B. 10'
    C. 12'
    D. 15'

12._____are not marked in any way to identify the frequency or location of temporary installation restraint/bracing.

     A. Sheathing
     B. Web member
     C. Trusses
     D. Blocking

13. What kind of bending should be avoided when unloading trusses?

     A. 90°
     B. 45°
     C. lateral
     D. None of the above

14._____size should be determined by weight and size of trusses to be hoisted.

     A. Roof
     B. Crane
     C. Spreader bar
     D. Hoist

15. How many lift points should you have for truss bundles with Top Chord Pitch greater than 60 degrees?

     A. 10
     B. 5
     C. 8
     D. 3

16._____ ground bracing tie off trusses to a series of braces that are attached to stakes driven the ground.

     A. Lateral
     B. Diagonal
     C. Exterior
     D. Interior

17._____ plane requires temporary/permanent diagonal bracing.

     A. Truss
     B. Blocking
     C. Girders
     D. Web member

How often should you cut or drill a structural member of a Truss?

A. As needed
B. Always
C. Never
D. None of the above

_____ is/are the horizontal distance(s) between outside edges of exterior bearings.

A. Panel points
B. Continuous lateral span
C. Truss spacings
D. Truss span

What is truss heel height?

A. Vertical length at the outside face of bearing
B. Vertical length at the inside face of bearing
C. Vertical depth at the outside face of bearing
D. Vertical depth at the inside face of bearing

What are trusses specially designed to carry extra loads from framing and equipment? Girders

A. Girders
B. Mono truss
C. Scissor truss
D. Parallel chord trusses

Toe_____ is often used to connect corner and end jack trusses together.

A. Truss
B. Bracing
C. Joint
D. Nailing

_____ is a solid member placed between structural members, usually at the bearings.

A. 2 x 4
B. Backing
C. Blocking
D. Fire stop

24._____ is a roof having 2 slopes on each side of the peak , the lower slope usually steeper than the upper.

     A. Scissor
     B. Parallel
     C. Gambrel
     D. None of the above

25. For 2 x 6 or greater lateral restraint and diagonal bracing, use a minimum of _____?

     A. 4 nail
     B. 3 nails
     C. 2 nails
     D. 1 nail

Problem Set #1:

A	Page 8, Figure B1-10B and Figure B1-11A&B
D	Page 6
B	Page 9
B	Page 11
C	Page 11
C	Page 15
A	Page 19
A	Page 27
D	Page 53
C	Page 55
D	Page 79
C	Page 2
C	Page 3
B	Page 4
D	Page 7
C	Page 10
D	Page 13
C	Page 16
D	Page 96
C	Page 95
A	Page 69
D	Page 66
C	Page 91
C	Page 92, 22 Figure 82-15
B	Page 61, Figure B7-13

Gypsum Construction Handbook, 7th Ed.
Questions and Answers

1. _____ fastener should be used when 3/8", ½" and 5/8" single layer gypsum panels are attached to wood framing.

   A. 1-1/2" Type G bugle head
   B. 1-1/4 Type S bugle head
   C. 1-1/8" Type S bugle head
   D. 1-1/4" Type W bugle head

2. _____ is/are warning signs of fastener imperfections.

   A. Darkening
   B. Localized cracking
   C. Protrusion of the fasteners
   D. All of the above

3. Extended periods of _____ will discolor panel face paper.

   A. High humidity
   B. Low humidity
   C. Cold weather
   D. Strong sunlight

4. ⅜-inch gypsum panels are designed for framing centers up to _____.

   A. 24 inches
   B. 16 inches
   C. 20 inches
   D. 12 inches

5. _____ is often caused by excessively fast drying of joint compounds.

   A. Loose panels
   B. Board sagging
   C. Joint cracking
   D. None of the above

6. Use _____ screw to connect ¾ inch single-layer panels to steel studs.

   A. 1 inch Type S bugle head
   B. 1⅛ inch Type S bugle head
   C. 1¼ inch Type S bugle head
   D. 2¼ inch Type S bugle head

Stack panels face up with ends resting on nominal 2" x 4" lumber and with center of the boards resting on floor, and allow to remain overnight or until they have _____ .

A. A 1" space between adjacent panels
B. At least a 2" permanent bow
C. No stains or discoloration on face paper
D. All of the above

Maintain and control heat in the range of 55°F to 70°F 24 hours _____ the entire gypsum board finishing process.

A. Before
B. During
C. After
D. All of the above

Board sags in ceiling are often caused by _____ .

A. Improperly fitted panels
B. Insufficient support of board
C. High-humid conditions
D. All of the above

Long partition runs shall have _____ to compensate for hygrometric and thermal expansion.

A. Relief joints
B. Expansion joints
C. All the above
D. Control joints

All but _____ will cause cracking of compound joints in veneer plaster finishing.

A. Maximum air circulation
B. Rapid drying
C. Possible shrinkage
D. All of the above

Maximum frame spacing for ⅜ inch single-layer ceiling application is _____ o.c.

A. 12 inches
B. 16 inches
C. 24 inches
D. In compliance with local building codes

Where single-nailing is used, drive nails at least _____ inch(es) from ends or edges of gypsum board.

A. ¼ inch
B. ⅝ inch
C. ½ inch
D. ⅜ inch

14. Joint defects generally occur in a straight-line pattern and in most cases result from _____.

   A. Incorrect framing
   B. Incorrect joint treatment
   C. Climatic conditions
   D. All of the above

15. Wood furring strips over wood framing shall be _____ minimum size for nail-on application.

   A. 1" x 1"
   B. 1" x 2"
   C. 1" x 3"
   D. 2" x 2"

16. It is desirable to limit deflection to _____ and never exceed L/120 for drywall assemblies.

   A. L/120
   B. L/180
   C. L/240
   D. L/360

17. According to *The Gypsum Construction Handbook*, a drywall hammer is used to _____

   A. compress gypsum panel face and leave desired dimple
   B. wedge panels
   C. pry panels
   D. All of the above

18. The screw must enter perpendicular to the board face for proper performance, drive screws at least _____ from ends or edges of the gypsum board.

   A. ¼ inch
   B. ⅜ inch
   C. ½ inch
   D. ⅝ inch

19. A board sagging between ceiling support is caused by _____.

   A. Improper ventilation
   B. Extended exposure to strong sunlight
   C. Low humidity
   D. High humidity

20. A minimum temperature of _____ should be maintained during gypsum board application.

   A. 45° F
   B. 50° F
   C. 55° F
   D. 70° F

Gypsum products may not be stored in temperatures that exceed _____ F.

A. 115°
B. 125°
C. 130°
D. 135°

Tape overlapped at joint intersections _____ in veneer plaster.

A. Is recommended to strengthen the joints
B. Is only recommended when the joints are at angles
C. Is only recommended if the joints are out of alignment
D. Can cause joint cracking

_____ of panels may be subject to scuffing and may develop paper bond failure or paper delamination from the gypsum core after application.

A. Board sag
B. Too much adhesive
C. Water damage
D. Strong sunlight

Where gypsum panels are attached to furring channels use _____ screw.

A. Type S bugle head
B. Type S-12 trim head
C. Type W bugle head
D. Type G bugle head

Firecode C Core gypsum panels are available in lengths of _____ feet.

A. 8, 9, 10, 12
B. 8, 10, 14, 16
C. 8, 9, 10, 12, 14
D. 9, 10, 12, 14

Maintain a minimum temperature of _____ during gypsum board application.

A. 30° F
B. 40° F
C. 50° F
D. 60° F

_____, to prevent joint darkening.

A. Always use white paint in finishing
B. Always finish joints in humid conditions
C. Be sure joints are thoroughly dry before painting
D. None of the above

28. _____ after joint treatment are signs of edge cracking.

    A. Straight narrow cracks along edges of tape
    B. Cracks along edges of door and/or window opening
    C. Cracks on edges of any curved application
    D. Cracks along sides of pre-finished panels

29. In large ceiling areas, _____ are recommended to relieve internal stress buildup.

    A. Control joints
    B. Seismic joints
    C. Cladding joints
    D. Stress joints

30. Structural movement and most cracking problems are caused by _____.

    A. Change in materials due to temperature and humidity changes
    B. Deflection under load
    C. Seismic forces
    D. All of the above

31. _____ systems consist of reinforcing tape and joint compound.

    A. Reinforcing
    B. Joint treatment
    C. Finishing
    D. Bonding

32. When installing wood studs and joists, apply gypsum boards first _____.

    A. To the ceiling and then to the walls
    B. To bottom of wall, then top of wall, then ceiling
    C. To walls first in any order, then to ceiling
    D. Parallel, in any order

33. Joint compounds and textures are seriously affected by lower temperatures; _____.

    A. Suffer loss of strength
    B. Loss of bond
    C. Crack from thermal shock
    D. All of the above

34. Where screw application is used for attaching gypsum panel to either wood or steel framing, screwhead shall be driven _____ but not deep enough to break the paper.

    A. To just above
    B. Flush with
    C. Slightly below the face of the panel
    D. Deep enough to just slightly break

_____ screw is used to attach ½ inch or ⅝ inches of single-layer gypsum panel and base to steel framing.

A. 1 inch Bugle Head Type S
B. 1 ⅛ inch Bugle Head Type S
C. 1 ¼ inch Bugle Head Type S
D. 1 ⅝ inch Bugle Head Type S

⅜-inch gypsum board applied with long dimension perpendicular to framing has a bending radius of _____ feet.

A. 20
B. 9.5
C. 6
D. 5

Certain interior wall surface should be isolated with surface control joints or other means where _____.

A. Construction changes within the plane of the wall
B. Tile and thin brick surfaces exceed 16 feet in either direction
C. A wall abuts a structural element or dissimilar wall
D. All of the above

Install gypsum products at comfortable working temperatures continuously _____ Fahrenheit.

A. Above 50°
B. Below 72°
C. Below 50°
D. None of the above

_____, gypsum panels can be prebowed and adhesively attached with fasteners at the top and bottom only.

A. When applied to a curved surface
B. When it is determined that humidity will warm them
C. Where fasteners at the vertical joints are objectionable
D. None of the above

_____ screws are used to attach ½ inch gypsum board to metal studs.

A. Type A
B. Type S
C. Type W
D. Type G

_____ is not recommended as a base for ceramic or other tile.

A. USG Sheetrock Regular Core
B. Durock brand cement board
C. USG Fiberock Brand Aqua-Tough Interior Panels
D. Fiberock Aqua-Tough tile backerboard

42. ¼" drywall is typically used for _____.

   A. Joint treatment
   B. Curved walls
   C. Stress joints
   D. Both A and B

43. _____ gypsum panel complies with ASTM requirements for Type X gypsum board.

   A. Moisture resistant
   B. Curved walls
   C. Fire resistant
   D. Stress resistant

44. Gypsum board that is green in color is known as _____.

   A. Stress resistant
   B. Moisture resistant
   C. Fire resistant
   D. Dirt resistant

45. One of the most effective, lowest cost methods of reducing sound transmission when installing drywall is _____.

   A. Curved walls
   B. Fire resistant
   C. Resilient channel
   D. None of the above

46. When fastening steel studs to runners, _____ fastener is required.

   A. Type S pan head
   B. Type T pan head
   C. Type W pan head
   D. Type G pan head

47. When installing resilient channel, _____ fastener is required.

   A. 1¼" Type W
   B. Type S bugle head screws
   C. ¼" drywall
   D. Both A and B

48. When installing 5/8" gypsum panels to wood studs, the minimum length screw required is a _____.

   A. 1½" Type G bugle head
   B. 1¼" Type S bugle head
   C. 1⅛" Type S bugle head
   D. 1¼" Type W Bugle Head

When attaching steel framing components to poured concrete and block surfaces, _____ fastener is required.

A. Standard
B. Tapcon
C. Stress joint
D. Type S

When single layer drywall board is applied over metal studs, _____ fastener is used.

A. 2½" Type S
B. 1¼" Type W
C. 1" Type S
D. 1½" Type G

_____ is the minimum length drywall screw used for installing 5/8" drywall to wood studs.

A. 1¼"
B. 1"
C. ¾"
D. 2"

_____ is the thickest drywall you can install using a 1½" annular drywall nail.

A. 1"
B. 2"
C. ¾"
D. 1¼"

_____ joint compound drywall hardens quick enough to provide same day finishing.

A. Fire resistant
B. Powder setting
C. Standard setting
D. Moisture resistant

It will take _____ gallons of joint compound to cover 1,000 square feet of drywall.

A. 3.8
B. 10.2
C. 9.4
D. 8.4

The metal furring channels should be attached to bar joists with a furred ceiling _____.

A. 14" on center maximum, at right angles to the bar joists
B. 12" on center maximum, at right angles to the bar joists
C. 24" on center maximum, at right angles to the bar joists
D. 28" on center maximum, at right angles to the bar joists

56. When framing a ceiling _____ is the maximum span for ½" single layer panels in one span using 25 metal furring channels with 16" o.c. spacing.

   A. 5'9"
   B. 3'5"
   C. 6'4"
   D. 4'9"

57. According to the *Gypsum Construction Handbook*, which of the following is the safest way to store gypsum panel products on the jobsite where the storage area has already been determined to be a large dry room and the floor load limit is able to accommodate a concentrated point load of gypsum panels?

   A. stacked flat on risers in the center of the room
   B. on edge leaning against the wall framing with warning tape or signage
   C. in vertical stacks around the sides of the room with at least 3 inches of space between the bottom of the first board in the stack and the wall
   D. in vertical stacks around the sides of the room with at least 8 inches of space between the bottom of the first board in the stack and the wall and warning tape or signage

58. _____ is the minimum temperature you can apply to joint compound.

   A. 45° F
   B. 35° F
   C. 50° F
   D. 55° F

59. _____ is the minimum temperature at which you can hang sheetrock.

   A. 45° F
   B. 55° F
   C. 66° F
   D. 50° F

60. When installing sheetrock, you stay_____ from the edges with the drywall screws.

   A. 3/8"
   B. 1/8"
   C. 7/8"
   D. 3/5"

61. When placing sheetrock over wood framing, first _____.

   A. Apply gypsum to the corner, then to the center
   B. Apply gypsum to the ceiling, then to the wall
   C. Apply gypsum to the wall, then to the ceiling
   D. None of the above

When installing sheetrock over wood framing, _____, is the proper arrangement of drywall joints.

A. To the ceiling and then to the walls
B. Arrange joints on opposite sides of partition so they occur on different studs
C. To bottom of wall, then top of wall, then ceiling
D. None of the above

With gypsum multi-layer adhesive applications, the joints should be offset a minimum of _____ inches.

A. 12
B. 20
C. 10
D. 15

When installing gypsum in soffit areas, a control joint should be installed _____.

A. A maximum of 30 feet
B. A minimum of 40 feet
C. A maximum of 10 feet
D. A minimum of 50 feet

_____ is used to reinforce the outside corners of sheetrock.

A. Joint compound
B. Corner bead
C. Bonding
D. Resilient channel

When fastening 200-A & 200-B metal trim to drywall, _____ is the spacing of the nails.

A. 10" on-center
B. 9" off-center
C. 7" on-center
D. 9" on-center

When drywall fasteners are replaced, the heads of the screws should be covered with _____.

A. Joint compound
B. Curved wall
C. Corner bead
D. Bonding

¼" and ⅜" sheetrock are NOT recommended for _____.

A. Curved walls
B. Sound control
C. Joint compound
D. Resilient channel

Gypsum Construction Handbook, 7th Ed.
Answers

A.M. 06/29/2020

1.	D	Page 39
2.	D	Page 370
3.	D	Page 355
4.	B	Page 3
5.	C	Page 370
6.	C	Page 38
7.	B	Page 112
8.	D	Page 103
9.	D	Page 371
10.	D	Page 358
11.	D	Page 355
12.	B	Page 73
13.	D	Page 108
14.	D	Page 370
15.	D	Page 90
16.	C	Page 70
17.	A	Page 424
18.	B	Page 110
19.	D	Page 353
20.	B	Page 105
21.	B	Page 3
22.	D	Page 386
23.	C	Page 372
24.	A	Page 124
25.	C	Page 9
26.	C	Page 105
27.	C	Page 383/392
28.	A	Page 380
29.	A	Page 355
30.	D	Page 354
31.	B	Page 52
32.	A	Page 113
33.	D	Page 354
34.	C	Page 107
35.	A	Page 42
36.	C	Page 136
37.	D	Page 148/149
38.	A	Page 354
39.	C	Page 112
40.	B	Page 36
41.	A	Page 3 and 6
42.	B	Page 5
43.	C	Page 5
44.	B	Page 7
45.	C	Page 31

International Residential Code, 2021
Chapters 1 and 44 Administration and Referenced Standards
Questions and Answers

1. The *International Residential Code* is applicable to single-family dwellings a maximum of _____ stories in above-grade-plane height.

    A. One
    B. Two
    C. Three
    D. Four

2. If there is a conflict in the code between a general requirement and a specific requirement, the _____ requirement shall apply.

    A. General
    B. Specific
    C. Least restrictive
    D. Most restrictive

3. Provisions of the appendices do not apply unless _____.

    A. Specified in the code
    B. Applicable to unique conditions
    C. Specifically reference in the adopting ordinance
    D. Relevant to fire or life safety

4. _____ is the term used in the IRC to describe the individual in charge of the department of building safety.

    A. Building official
    B. Code official
    C. Code administrator
    D. Chief building inspector

5. The building official has the authority to _____ the provisions of the code.

    A. Ignore
    B. Waive
    C. Violate
    D. Interpret

6. Used materials may be utilized under which one of the following conditions?

    A. They meet the requirements for new materials
    B. When approved by the building official
    C. Used materials may never be used in new construction
    D. A representative sampling is tested for compliance

7. The building official has the authority to grant modifications to the code _____.

    A. For only those issues not affecting life safety or fire safety
    B. For individual cases where the strict letter of the code is impractical
    C. Where the intent and purpose of the code cannot be met
    D. Related only to administrative functions

8. Unless supporting a surcharge, retaining walls having a maximum height of _____ feet, measured from the bottom of the footing to the top of the wall, do not require a permit.

    A. 2
    B. 3
    C. 4
    D. 5

9. Tests performed by _____ may be required by the building official where there is insufficient evidence of code compliance.

    A. The owner
    B. The contractor
    C. An approved agency
    D. A design professional

10. Other than storm shelters, a permit is not required for the construction of a one-story detached accessory structure when it has a maximum floor area of _____ square feet.

    A. 100
    B. 120
    C. 150
    D. 200

11. Prefabricated swimming pools are subject to a building permit where they have a minimum depth of _____ inches.

    A. 12
    B. 24
    C. 30
    D. 36

12. Unless an extension is authorized, a permit becomes invalid when work does not commence within _____ after permit issuance.

    A. 90 days
    B. 180 days
    C. One year
    D. Two years

13. The building permit, or a copy of the permit, shall be kept _____ until completion of the project

    A. At the job site
    B. By the permit applicant
    C. By the contractor
    D. By the owner

14. When a building permit is issued, the construction documents shall be approved _____.

    A. In writing or by stamp
    B. And two sets returned to the applicant
    C. And stamped as "accepted as reviewed"
    D. Pending payment of the plan review fee

15. Unless otherwise mandated by state or local laws, the approved construction documents shall be retain by the building official for a minimum of _____ from the date of completion of the permitted work.

    A. 90 days
    B. 180 days
    C. One year
    D. Two years

16. _____ inspections are not specifically identified by the *International Residential Code* as a required inspection.

    A. Foundation
    B. Frame
    C. Fire-resistance-construction
    D. Energy efficiency

17. It is the duty of the _____ to provide access to work in need of inspection.

    A. The permit holder or agent
    B. The owner or owner's agent
    C. The contractor
    D. The person requesting the inspection

18. The certificate of occupancy shall contain all of the following information except _____.

    A. The name and address of the owner or owner's agent
    B. The name of the building official
    C. The edition of the code under which the permit was issued
    D. The maximum occupant load

19. A temporary certificate of occupancy is valid for _____.

   A. 30 days
   B. 60 days
   C. 180 days
   D. A period set by the building official

20. The board of appeals is not authorized to rule on an appeal based on a claim that _____.

   A. The provisions of the code do not fully apply
   B. A code requirement should be waived
   C. The rules have been incorrectly interpreted
   D. A better form of construction is provided

21. The membership of the board of appeals _____.

   A. Shall include a jurisdictional member
   B. Must consist of at least five members
   C. Shall be knowledgeable of building construction
   D. Must include an engineer or an architect

22. A permit is not required for construction of a fence with a maximum height of _____ feet.

   A. 5
   B. 6
   C. 7
   D. 8

23. When a stop work order is issued, it shall be given to any of the following individuals except for the _____.

   A. Owner
   B. Owner's agent
   C. Permit applicant
   D. Person doing the work

24. Standard _____ is applicable for factory-built fireplaces.

   A. ANSI z21.42-2014
   B. CPSC 16 CFR Part 1404
   C. NFPA 259-13
   D. UL 127–2011

25. ACI 318-19 is a reference standard addressing _____.

   A. Structural concrete
   B. Wood construction
   C. Structural steel buildings
   D. Gypsum board

26. All of the following issues are specifically identified for achieving the purpose of the *International Residential Code*, except for _____.

    A. Affordability
    B. Structural strength
    C. Energy conservation
    D. Usability and accessibility

27. A permit is not required for the installation of a window awning provided the awning projects a maximum of _____ inches from the exterior wall and does not require additional support.

    A. 30
    B. 36
    C. 48
    D. 54

28. Where a self-contained refrigeration system contains a maximum of _____ pound(s) of refrigerant, a permit is not required.

    A. 1
    B. 2
    C. 5
    D. 10

29. It is the duty of the _____ or their agent to notify the building official that work is ready for inspection.

    A. Permit holder
    B. Owner
    C. Contractor
    D. Design professional

30. What is the role of the building official in relationship to the board of appeals?

    A. Advisor only
    B. Ex officio member
    C. Full voting member
    D. Procedural reviewer

31. Where the enforcement of a code provision would violate the conditions of an appliance's listing, the conditions of the listing _____.

    A. Are no longer valid
    B. May be disregarded
    C. Shall apply
    D. Are optional

32. Inspection reports shall be retained in the official records for _____.

    A. Until after the certificate of occupancy is issued
    B. 180 days after the report is issued
    C. The time required for the retention of public records
    D. 180 days after the certificate of occupancy is issued

33. Which of the following reasons is not specifically identified by the code as authority to suspend or revoke a permit?

    A. The permit was issued in error
    B. Required inspections have not been performed
    C. It was issued in violation of a jurisdictional ordinance
    D. Inaccurate information was provided at the time of issuance

34. A permit for a temporary structure is limited as to time of service but shall not be allowed for more than _____ days.

    A. 30
    B. 60
    C. 90
    D. 180

35. The issuance of a certificate of occupancy is not required for accessory building's whose total area is less than _____.

    A. 120 square feet
    B. 150 square feet
    C. 180 square feet
    D. All accessory buildings are exempt

Please see Answer Key on the following page
ABC 08/19/2021

International Residential Code, 2021
Chapters 1 and 44 Administration and Referenced Standards
Answer Key

	Answer	**Section/Page #**
1.	C	101.2
2.	B	102.1
3.	C	102.5
4.	A	103.1
5.	D	104.1
6.	B	104.9.1
7.	B	104.10
8.	C	105.2, Building #3
9.	C	104.11.1
10.	D	105.2, Building #1
11.	B	105.2, Building #7
12.	B	105.5
13.	A	105.7
14.	A	106.3.1
15.	B	106.5
16.	D	109.1 – 109.1.6
17.	D	109.3
18.	D	110.3
19.	D	110.4
20.	B	112.2
21.	C	112.3
22.	C	105.2, Building #2
23.	C	114.2
24.	D	44-35
25.	A	44-2
26.	D	101.3
27.	D	105.2, Building #9
28.	D	105.2, Mechanical #7
29.	A	109.3
30.	B	112.1
31.	C	102.4, Exception
32.	C	104.7
33.	B	105.6
34.	D	107.1
35.	D	110.1, Exception 2

International Residential Code, 2021
Sections R301 and R302
Questions and Answers

1. The weathering potential for all dwelling sites located in the state of South Dakota is _____.

   A. Severe
   B. Moderate
   C. Negligible
   D. None

2. Based on Figure R301.2 (3), the ground snow load for most of western Colorado is _____.

   A. 30 psf
   B. 40 psf
   C. 50 psf
   D. Site-specific due to extreme local variations

3. Unless local conditions warrant otherwise, the probability for termite infestation for dwellings constructed in most of Idaho is _____.

   A. Very heavy
   B. Moderate to heavy
   C. Slight to moderate
   D. None to slight

4. For the purpose of determining the component and cladding loads on the roof surface of a building, the area at the ridge of a gable roof sloped at 20 degrees shall be considered as Pressure Zone _____ at other than the eaves.

   A. 0
   B. 1
   C. 2
   D. 3

5. Where wood structural panels are used to protect windows in buildings located in windborne debris regions, #8 wood screws shall be located at a maximum of _____ inches on center to fasten those panels that span 8 feet.

   A. 8
   B. 9
   C. 12
   D. 16

6. Where a referenced document is based upon nominal design wind speeds and no conversion between ultimate design wind speeds and nominal design wind speeds is provided, an ultimate design wind speed of 115 mph shall be converted to a nominal design wind speed of _____ mph.

   A. 85
   B. 89
   C. 93
   D. 101

7. The wind exposure category appropriate for a dwelling located in a residential development in a suburban area is _____.

   A. Exposure A
   B. Exposure B
   C. Exposure C
   D. Exposure D

8. The seismic design category for a site having a calculated S_{DS} of 0.63g is _____.

   A. B
   B. D_0
   C. D_1
   D. E

9. Habitable attics shall be designed with a minimum uniformly distributed live load of _____ psf.

   A. 10
   B. 20
   C. 30
   D. 40

10. For a dwelling assigned to Seismic Design Category D_2 and constructed under the conventional provisions of the IRC, the maximum dead load permitted for 8-inch-thick masonry walls is _____ psf.

    A. 40
    B. 65
    C. 80
    D. 85

11. A portion of a building is considered irregular for seismic purposes when a floor opening, such as for stairway, exceeds the lesser of 12 feet or _____ percent of the least floor dimension.

    A. 15
    B. 25
    C. 33 1/3
    D. 50

12. Buildings constructed in regions where the ground snow load exceeds a minimum of _____ psf must be designed in accordance with accepted engineering practice.

    A. 30
    B. 50
    C. 70
    D. 90

13. For rooms other than sleeping rooms, the minimum uniformly distributed live load that is to be used for the design of the floor system is _____ psf.

    A. 20
    B. 30
    C. 40
    D. 50

14. A minimum uniformly distributed live load of 10 psf is to be used for the design of uninhabitable attic areas having a maximum clear height of _____ inches.

    A. 30
    B. 36
    C. 42
    D. 60

15. A minimum uniformly distributed live load of _____ psf shall be used for the design of sleeping rooms.

    A. 10
    B. 20
    C. 30
    D. 40

16. Where no snow load is present, the minimum roof design live load for a 240 square foot tributary-loaded roof area having a slope of 8:12 is _____ psf.

    A. 20
    B. 16
    C. 14
    D. 12

17. The maximum allowable deflection for floors is _____.

    A. L/120
    B. L/180
    C. L/240
    D. L/360

18. The maximum allowable deflection permitted for 7:12-sloped rafters with no finished ceiling attached the rafters is _____.

    A. L/120
    B. L/180
    C. L/240
    D. L/360

19. A fire-resistance rating is not required for exterior walls of nonsprinklered dwellings having a minimu fire separation distance of _____ feet.

    A. 3
    B. 4
    C. 5
    D. 10

20. A roof projection on a dwelling shall be located a minimum of _____ foot/feet from an interior line.

    A. 0 (it may extend to the lot line)
    B. 1
    C. 2
    D. 4

21. Tool and storage sheds, playhouses and similar accessory structures having a maximum floor area of _____ square feet are not required to have exterior wall protection based on location on the lot.

    A. 100
    B. 120
    C. 150
    D. 200

22. Walls and ceiling finishes shall have a maximum flame spread index of _____.

    A. 25
    B. 75
    C. 200
    D. 450

23. Penetrations shall be protected by an approved penetration firestop system installed with a positive pressure differential of not less than _____ inch of water.

    A. 0.05
    B. 0.03
    C. 0.1
    D. 0.01

24. Where a detached garage is located within 2 feet of a lot line, the maximum eave projection is limited to _____ inches.

    A. 4
    B. 6
    C. 8
    D. 12

25. For wind design purposes, a building located along the shoreline in the Great Lakes region is categorized as Exposure _____ where exposed to wind coming from over the water.

    A. A
    B. B
    C. C
    D. D

26. A _____ is exempt from the seismic requirements of the code.

    A. Townhouse in Seismic Design Category C
    B. One-family dwelling in Seismic Design Category C
    C. Townhouse in Seismic Design Category D_0
    D. Two-family dwelling in Seismic Design Category D_1

27. Where a solid wood door is installed as a permitted opening between a garage and a residence, the minimum thickness of the door shall be _____ inches.

    A. 1 3/8
    B. 1 ½
    C. 1 5/8
    D. 1 ¾

28. When a common wall is used to separate townhouses provided with fire sprinkler protection, it shall have a minimum _____-hour-fire-resistance rating.

    A. 1
    B. 2
    C. 3
    D. 4

29. An in-fill panel for a guard shall be designed to withstand a minimum load of _____ pounds applied horizontally on an area of 1 square foot.

    A. 50
    B. 80
    C. 100
    D. 200

30. Where structural wood panels are used to provide windborne debris protection for glazed openings, the fasteners shall be long enough to penetrate through the sheathing and into wood wall framing a minimum of _____ inch(es).

    A. 1
    B. 1 ½
    C. 2
    D. 2 ½

31. In the determination of the allowable deflection for cantilevered structural members, "L" shall be taken as _____ length of the cantilever.

    A. The actual
    B. 1 ½ times the
    C. Twice the
    D. 3 times the

32. Attic spaces served by a fixed stair shall be designed to support a minimum live load of _____ p

    A. 10
    B. 20
    C. 30
    D. 40

33. Unless listed for lesser clearances, combustible insulation shall be separated a minimum of _____ inch(es) from recessed luminaires, fan motors and other heat-producing devices.

    A. 1
    B. 3
    C. 4
    D. 6

34. The aggregate area of openings in an exterior wall of a nonsprinklered dwelling located with a fire separation distance of four feet is limited to a maximum of _____ percent of the exterior wall ar

    A. 10
    B. 25
    C. 50
    D. 100

Please see Answer Key on the following page

ABC 08/20/2021

International Residential Code, 2021
Sections R301 and R302 – Questions and Answers
Answer Key

	Answer	Section #
1.	A	Figure 301.2(1) Weathering Probability Map for Concrete
2.	D	Figure 301.2(3) Ground Snow Loads for The United States
3.	C	Figure 318.4 Termite Infestation Probability Map
4.	C	Figure 301.2.1 Component and Cladding Pressure Zones
5.	A	Table 301.2.1.2 Windborne Debris Protection Fastening Schedule for Wood Structural Panels
6.	B	Table 301.2.1.3 Wind Speed Conversions
7.	B	301.2.1.4
8.	B	Table 301.2.2.1.1 Seismic Design Category Determination
9.	C	Table 301.5 Minimum Uniformly Distributed Live Loads
10.	C	301.2.2.2
11.	D	301.2.2.6
12.	C	301.2.3
13.	C	Table 301.5 Minimum Uniformly Distributed Live Loads
14.	C	Table 301.5 Minimum Uniformly Distributed Live Loads (Note b)
15.	C	Table 301.5 Minimum Uniformly Distributed Live Loads
16.	C	Table 301.6 Minimum Roof Live Loads in Pounds-Force Per Square Foot of Horizontal Projection
17.	D	Table 301.7 Allowable Deflection of Structural Members
18.	B	Table 301.7 Allowable Deflection of Structural Members
19.	C	Table 302.1(1) Exterior Walls
20.	C	Tables 302.1(1) Exterior Walls
21.	D	302.l, Exception 3 105.2, Building 1
22.	C	302.9.1
23.	D	302.4.1.2
24.	A	302.l, Exception 4
25.	D	301.2.1.4
26.	B	301.2.2
27.	A	302.5.1
28.	A	302.2.2
29.	A	Table 301.5 Minimum Uniformly Distributed Live Loads (Note f)
30.	C	Table 301.2.1.2, Windborne Debris Protection Fastening Schedule for Wood Structural Panels (Note c)
31.	C	Table 301.7 Allowable Deflection of Structural Members (Note b)
32.	C	Table 301.5 Minimum Uniformly Distributed Live Loads
33.	B	302.14
34.	B	Table 302.1(1)

International Residential Code, 2021
Sections R303 - R310
Questions and Answers

1. When natural light is used to satisfy the minimum light requirements for habitable rooms, the aggregate glazing area shall be a minimum of _____ percent of the floor area.

    A. 4
    B. 5
    C. 8
    D. 10

2. When natural ventilation is used to satisfy the minimum ventilation requirements for habitable rooms, the aggregate open area to the outdoors shall be a minimum of _____ percent of the floor area.

    A. 4
    B. 5
    C. 8
    D. 10

3. Garage sprinklers, when required, shall be residential sprinklers or quick-response sprinklers, designed to provide a density of _____ gpm/sf.

    A. 0.05
    B. 0.10
    C. 0.15
    D. 0.25

4. Where applicable escape and rescue openings are provided and a whole-house mechanical ventilation system is installed, glazing is not required for natural light purposes if artificial light is provided capable of producing an average illumination of _____ footcandle(s) over the area of the room at a height of 30 inches above the floor level.

    A. 1
    B. 5
    C. 6
    D. 10

5. Habitable rooms other than kitchens shall have a minimum floor area of _____ square feet.

    A. 70
    B. 100
    C. 120
    D. 150

6. The floor area beneath a furred ceiling can be considered to be contributing to the minimum required habitable area for the room where it has a minimum height of _____ above the floor.

    A. 5 feet
    B. 6 feet, 4 inches
    C. 6 feet, 8 inches
    D. 7 feet

7. Other than in a kitchen, the minimum permitted horizontal dimension of any habitable room is _____ feet.

    A. 6
    B. 7
    C. 8
    D. 9

8. In general, the minimum required ceiling height of all habitable rooms is _____.

    A. 6 feet, 8 inches
    B. 7 feet, 0 inches
    C. 7 feet, 6 inches
    D. 8 feet, 0 inches

9. Ceilings in portions of basements without habitable spaces shall have a minimum ceiling height of _____ from the finished floor to beams, ducts, or other obstructions.

    A. 6 feet, 4 inches
    B. 6 feet, 6 inches
    C. 6 feet, 8 inches
    D. 7 feet, 0 inches

10. A minimum clearance of _____ inches shall be provided in front of a water closet.

    A. 21
    B. 24
    C. 30
    D. 32

11. The minimum distance between the centerline of a water closet and a side wall shall be _____ inches.

    A. 15
    B. 16
    C. 18
    D. 21

12. Within a shower compartment, the walls shall be finished with a nonabsorbent surface to a minimum height of _____.

    A. 5
    B. 6
    C. 7
    D. 8

13. Complying heating facilities are not required in dwelling units where the winter design temperature of the locale is a minimum of _____.

    A. 60°F
    B. 64°F
    C. 68°F
    D. 70°F

14. Where located less than 5 feet above the walking surface, glazing in a wall enclosing an outdoor hot tu shall be considered to be installed in a hazardous location unless the glazing is less than _____ inches horizontally from the water's edge.

    A. 24
    B. 36
    C. 60
    D. 72

15. A skylight is defined by the IRC as glass or other glazing material installed at a minimum slope of _____.

    A. 15 degrees from the vertical
    B. 30 degrees from the vertical
    C. 15 degrees from the horizontal
    D. 30 degrees from the horizontal

16. Curbs are not required for skylights installed on roofs having a minimum slope of _____.

    A. 2:12
    B. 3:12
    C. 4:12
    D. 5:12

17. A screen used to protect an air exhaust opening that terminates outdoors shall have a minimum openir size of inch and a maximum opening size of _____ inch and a maximum opening size of _____ inch.

    A. 1/8, ¼
    B. ¼, 3/8
    C. ¼, ½
    D. ½, ¾

18. A minimum clearance of _____ inches shall be provided in front of the opening to a shower.

    A. 24
    B. 30
    C. 32
    D. 36

19. Regular glass used in a louvered window shall be a minimum of _____ inch in nominal thickness.

    A. 3/32
    B. 1/8
    C. 5/32
    D. 3/16

20. Emergency escape and rescue openings shall have the bottom of the clear opening not greater than _____ inches above the floor.

    A. 40
    B. 42
    C. 44
    D. 48

21. Emergency escape and rescue openings, when considered as grade floor openings, shall have a minimum net clear opening of _____ square feet.

    A. 4.0
    B. 4.4
    C. 5.0
    D. 5.7

22. For an emergency escape and rescue opening, the minimum clear opening height shall be _____ inches, and the minimum clear opening width shall be _____ inches.

    A. 24, 20
    B. 24, 28
    C. 28, 22
    D. 28, 24

23. Where a window well is required in conjunction with an escape and rescue opening, the window well shall have a minimum net clear area of _____ square feet with a minimum horizontal dimension of _____ inches.

    A. 5.7, 20
    B. 5.7, 24
    C. 9.0, 30
    D. 9.0, 36

24. An asphalt surface is permitted as the floor surface of a carport provided the surface is _____.

    A. Limited to 400 square feet
    B. Located at ground level
    C. Sealed with an approved material
    D. Sloped a minimum of 1:48

25. A 6-square-foot skylight of laminated glass shall have a minimum _____-inch polyvinyl butyra interlayer where located 14 feet above the walking surface.

    A. 0.015
    B. 0.024
    C. 0.030
    D. 0.044

26. Unless located at least 3 feet below the contaminant source, a mechanical outside air intake opening shall be located a minimum of _____ feet from a plumbing vent.

    A. 3
    B. 5
    C. 10
    D. 12

27. The illumination source for interior stairs shall be capable of illuminating the treads and landings to a minimum level of _____ foot-candle(s).

    A. 1
    B. 5
    C. 8
    D. 10

28. A shower shall have a minimum ceiling height of _____ above an area of not less than 30 inche by 30 inches at the showerhead.

    A. 6 feet, 6 inches
    B. 6 feet, 8 inches
    C. 6 feet, 10 inches
    D. 7 feet, 0 inches

29. Glazing adjacent to a door to a storage closet is not required to be safety glazing provided the closet i: maximum of _____ feet in depth.

    A. 2
    B. 2.5
    C. 3
    D. 4

30. Glazing in a door shall be safety glazing where the opening allows the passage of a minimum _____-inch sphere.

    A. 3
    B. 3 ½
    C. 4
    D. 6

31. Where window wells are provided for escape and rescue openings, window well drainage is not required where the building foundation is supported by Group _____ soils.

    A. I
    B. I or II
    C. I, II, or III
    D. IV

32. Where lighting outlets are installed in interior stairways, a wall switch shall be provided at each floor level to control the light outlet where the stairway has a minimum of _____ risers.

    A. Two
    B. Three
    C. Four
    D. Six

33. A 4-square-foot glazed panel installed in an entry door shall have a minimum glazing category classification of CPSC 16 CFR 1201 Category _____.

    A. I
    B. II
    C. III
    D. IV

34. Except for storm shelters and those basements with a maximum floor area of _____ square feet used only to house mechanical equipment, all basements shall be provided with at least one operable emergency escape and rescue opening.

    A. 120
    B. 150
    C. 200
    D. 400

35. An emergency escape window may be installed under a deck or porch, provided a minimum height of _____ inches is maintained to a yard or court.

    A. 24
    B. 36
    C. 44
    D. 48

Please see Answer Key on the following page

International Residential Code, 2021
Sections R303 – R310 – Questions and Answers
Answer Key

	Answer	Section #
1.	C	303.1
2.	A	303.1
3.	A	309.5
4.	C	303.1, Exception 3
5.	A	304.1
6.	D	304.3
7.	B	304.2
8.	B	305.1
9.	A	305.1.1, Exception
10.	A	Figure 307.1 Minimum Fixture Clearances
11.	A	Figure 307.1 Minimum Fixture Clearances
12.	B	307.2
13.	A	303.10
14.	C	308.4.5
15.	A	308.6.1
		202, See "Skylights and Sloped Glazing"
16.	B	308.6.8
17.	C	303.6
18.	A	Figure 307.1 Minimum Fixture Clearances
19.	D	308.2
20.	C	310.2.3
21.	C	310.2.1, Exception
22.	A	310.2.2
23.	D	310.4.1
24.	B	309.2, Exception
25.	C	308.6.2
26.	C	303.5.1, Exception 1
27	A	303.7
28.	B	305.1, Exception 2
29.	C	308.4.2, Exception 3
30.	A	308.4.1, Exception 1
31.	A	310.4.3, Exception
32.	D	303.7
33.	A	Table 308.3.1(1) Minimum Category Classification of Glazing Using CPSC 16 CFR 1201
34.	C	310.1, Exception 1
35.	B	310.2.4

International Residential Code, 2021
Sections R311 - R323
Questions and Answers

1. The minimum width of a hallway shall be _____ feet.

    A. 2.5
    B. 3
    C. 3.5
    D. 4

2. Where the stairway has a straight run, a stairway landing shall have a minimum depth of _____ inches measured in the direction of travel.

    A. 30
    B. 32
    C. 36
    D. 42

3. Unless technically infeasible due to site constraints, the maximum slope of a ramp serving the required egress door shall be one-unit vertical in _____ units horizontal.

    A. Five
    B. Eight
    C. Ten
    D. Twelve

4. Handrails are not required on ramps having a maximum slope of _____.

    A. 1:5
    B. 1:8
    C. 1:12
    D. 1:15

5. Where a ramp changes direction, the width of the landing perpendicular to the ramp slope shall be a minimum of _____ inches.

    A. 36
    B. 42
    C. 48
    D. 60

6. Stairways shall be a minimum _____ inches wide at all points above the permitted handrail height and below the required headroom height.

    A. 30
    B. 34
    C. 36
    D. 38

7. Where a handrail is provided on one side of a stairway, the minimum required clear width at and below the handrail height is _____ inches.

    A. 27
    B. 29
    C. 31 ½
    D. 36

8. Stairways shall have a maximum riser height of _____ inches and a minimum tread run of _____ inches.

    A. 8 ¼, 9
    B. 8, 9
    C. 7 ¾, 10
    D. 7 ½, 10

9. The maximum variation between the greatest riser height and the smallest riser height within any flight of stairs shall be _____ inch.

    A. ¼
    B. 3/8
    C. ½
    D. 5/8

10. Unless a minimum tread depth of _____ inches is provided, a minimum 3/4-inch nosing is required at the leading edge of all treads.

    A. 9 ½
    B. 10
    C. 11
    D. 12

11. Unless the stair has a total rise of no more than 30 inches, the opening between treads at open risers shall be such that a minimum _____ sphere shall not pass through.

    A. 3-inch
    B. 4-inch
    C. 6-inch
    D. No limitation is mandated

12. In the identification of flood hazard areas, areas that have been determined to be subject to maximum wave heights of _____ feet are not required to be designated coastal high-hazard areas feet unless subject to high-velocity wave action or wave-induced erosion.

    A. 3
    B. 4
    C. 5
    D. 6

13. The maximum riser height permitted for spiral stairways is _____ inches.

    A. 7 ¾
    B. 8
    C. 8 ¼
    D. 9 ½

14. Stairway handrail height shall be, measured vertically from the nosing of the treads, a minimum of _____ inches and a maximum of _____ inches.

    A. 30, 34
    B. 30, 38
    C. 34, 38
    D. 34, 42

15. Where a stairway handrail is located adjacent to a wall, a minimum clearance of _____ inches shall be provided between the wall and the handrail.

    A. 1 ¼
    B. 1 ½
    C. 2
    D. 3 ½

16. A Type I handrail having a circular cross section shall have a minimum outside diameter of _____ inches and a maximum outside diameter of _____ inches.

    A. 1 ¼, 2
    B. 1 ¼, 2 5/8
    C. 1 ½, 2
    D. 1 ½, 2 5/8

17. A porch, balcony or similar raised floor surface more than 30 inches above the floor or grade below shall be provided with a guard having a minimum height of _____ inches.

    A. 32
    B. 34
    C. 36
    D. 42

18. Required guards on open sides of raised floor areas shall be provided with intermediate rails or ornamental closures such that a minimum _____-inch sphere cannot pass through.

    A. 3
    B. 4
    C. 6
    D. 9

19. Which one of the following areas in a dwelling unit does not specifically require the installation of a smoke alarm?

    A. Bathroom
    B. Kitchen
    C. Habitable attic
    D. Sleeping room

20. Where gypsum wallboard is used to separate foam plastic from the interior of the dwelling, the separation shall be minimum _____ gypsum board.

    A. ½ -inch
    B. ½-inch Type X
    C. 5/8-inch
    D. 5/85-inch Type X

21. When carbon monoxide alarms are required in new construction, they shall be installed _____.

    A. Within every bedroom
    B. On all floor levels of multistory units
    C. Outside of each separate sleeping area
    D. In the garage

22. An automatic residential fire sprinkler system shall be provided in all buildings containing _____ or more townhouses.

    A. All townhouses require a sprinkler system
    B. 8
    C. 16
    D. Sprinkler systems are not required in townhouses

23. In new construction, carbon monoxide alarms are required in dwelling units _____.

    A. Where fuel-fired appliances are installed
    B. That have attached garages with an opening to the dwelling
    C. With habitable space below grade
    D. Either a or b

24. Unless they are made of pressure preservative treated or naturally durable wood, wood framing members that rest on masonry or concrete exterior foundation walls shall be located a minimum of _____ inches from exposed ground.

    A. 6
    B. 8
    C. 12
    D. 18

25. In the establishment of a design flood elevation, the depth of peak elevation of flooding for a _____-year flood is used.

    A. 10
    B. 20
    C. 50
    D. 100

26. Where stair risers are not vertical, they shall be sloped under the tread above at a maximum angle of _____ from the vertical.

    A. 10°
    B. 15°
    C. 22°
    D. 30°

27. Where foam plastic is spray applied to a sill plate without a thermal barrier, it shall have a maximum density of _____ pcf.

    A. 1.0
    B. 1.5
    C. 2.0
    D. 3.0

28. The maximum width above the recess of a Type II handrail shall be _____ inches.

    A. 1 ½
    B. 2
    C. 2 5/8
    D. 2 ¾

29. Handrails shall be provided on at least one side of a stairway having a minimum of _____ risers.

    A. 2
    B. 3
    C. 4
    D. 5

30. The minimum required clear opening for an egress door from a dwelling unit is _____.

    A. 32 inches by 78 inches
    B. 32 inches by 80 inches
    C. 36 inches by 78 inches
    D. 36 inches by 80 inches

31. Where the door does not swing over the landing, the exterior landing at a required egress door shall be located a maximum of _____ inches below the top of the threshold.

    A. 7
    B. 7 ½
    C. 7 ¾
    D. 8

32. Where nosings are required on a stairway with solid risers, the nosings shall extend a minimum of _____ inch(es) and a maximum of _____ inch(es) beyond the risers.

    A. 1/2, 1
    B. ¾, 1 ¼
    C. 1, 1 ½
    D. 1 ¼, 2

33. Address numbers used for building identification shall have a minimum height of _____ inches.

    A. 4
    B. 6
    C. 8
    D. 9

34. Openings for required guards on the sides of stair treads shall be provided with intermediate rails or ornamental closures such that a minimum _____ sphere cannot pass through.

    A. 3 ½
    B. 4
    C. 4 3/8
    D. 6

35. Where a safe room is constructed as a storm shelter in order to provide safe refuge from high winds, the room shall be constructed in accordance with _____.

    A. ICC 500
    B. CPSC 16 CFR, Part 1201
    C. DOC PS 1-07
    D. FEMA TB-2-93

Please see Answer Key on the following page

International Residential Code, 2021
Sections R311 – R323 – Questions and Answers
Answer Key

	Answer	**Section #**
1.	B	311.6
2.	C	311.7.6
3.	D	311.8.1
4.	C	311.8.3
5.	A	311.8.2
6.	C	311.7.1
7.	C	311.7.1
8.	C	311.7.5.1, 311.7.5.2
9.	B	311.7.5.1
10.	C	311.7.5.3, Exception
11.	B	311.7.5.1
12.	A	322.3
13.	D	311.7.10.1
14.	C	311.7.8.1
15.	B	311.7.8.3
16.	A	311.7.8.5
17.	C	312.1.2
18.	B	312.1.3
19.	B	314.3
20.	A	316.4
21.	C	315.3
22.	A	313.1
23.	D	315.2.1
24.	B	317.1
25.	D	322.1.4
26.	D	311.7.5.1
27.	C	316.5.11
28.	D	311.7.8.5
29.	C	311.7.8
30.	A	311.2
31.	C	311.3.1, Exception
32.	B	311.7.5.3
33.	A	319.1
34.	C	312.1.3, Exception 2
35.	A	323.1

International Residential Code, 2021
Chapter 4
Questions and Answers

1. Unless grading is prohibited by physical barriers, lots shall be graded away from the foundation with minimum fall of _____ inches within the first _____ feet.

    A. 6, 5
    B. 6, 10
    C. 12, 5
    D. 12, 10

2. In the absence of a complete geotechnical evaluation to determine the soil's characteristics, clayey sand material shall be assumed to have a presumptive load-bearing value of _____ psf.

    A. 1,500
    B. 2,000
    C. 3,000
    D. 4,000

3. Concrete used in a basement slab shall have a minimum compressive strength of _____ psi when a severe weathering potential exists.

    A. 2,000
    B. 2,500
    C. 3,000
    D. 3,500

4. Air entrainment for concrete subjected to weathering, when required for locations other than garage floors with a steel troweled finish, shall have a total air content of _____ percent minimum and _____ percent maximum.

    A. 4, 7
    B. 4, 8
    C. 5, 7
    D. 5, 8

5. The minimum required width and thickness for concrete footings supporting light-frame construction a two-story 32-foot-wide house with a crawl space, in a locale with a 30 psf snow load and soil with a load-bearing value of 2000 is _____.

    A. 12 inches by 6 inches
    B. 13 inches by 6 inches
    C. 19 inches by 6 inches
    D. 24 inches by 7 inches

6. Where there is evidence that the groundwater table can rise to within _____ inch(es) of the finished floor at the building perimeter, the grade in the under-floor space shall be as high as the outside finished grade unless an approved drainage system is provided.

    A. 1
    B. 2
    C. 4
    D. 6

7. The minimum and maximum required footing projections for a concrete footing having a thickness of 8 inches are _____.

    A. 2 inches, 4 inches
    B. 2 inches, 8 inches
    C. 4 inches, 8 inches
    D. 8 inches, 12 inches

8. Where a permanent wood foundation basement wall system is used, the wall shall be supported by a minimum _____ footing plate resting on gravel or crushed stone fill a minimum of _____ inches in width.

    A. 2-inch-by-6-inch, 12
    B. 2-inch-by-8-inch, 16
    C. 2-inch-by-12-inch, 16
    D. 2-inch-by-12-inch, 24

9. For concrete foundation systems constructed in Seismic Design Category D2, foundations with stem walls shall be provided with a minimum of _____ bar(s) at the top of the wall and _____ bar(s) near the bottom of the footing.

    A. One #4, One #4
    B. One #5, One #5
    C. One #5, Two #4
    D. Two #4, Two #5

10. All exterior footings shall be placed a minimum of _____ inches below the undisturbed ground surface.

    A. 6
    B. 8
    C. 9
    D. 12

11. The maximum permitted slope for the bottom surface of footings shall be _____.

    A. 1:8
    B. 1:10
    C. 1:12
    D. 1:20

12. For a two-story dwelling assigned to Seismic Design Category B, anchor bolts used to attach wood sil plates to foundation walls shall be spaced a maximum of _____ feet on center.

    A. 4
    B. 5
    C. 6
    D. 7

13. Anchor bolts used to attach a wood sole plate to a concrete foundation shall be a minimum of _____ inch in diameter and extend a minimum of _____ inches into the concrete.

    A. ½, 7
    B. ½, 15
    C. 5/8, 7
    D. 5/8, 15

14. Soil described as a "sandy clay" has a Unified Soil Classification System Symbol of _____ and considered to be in Soil Group _____.

    A. SC, I
    B. CL, II
    C. SM, III
    D. CH, IV

15. In order to use frost protected shallow foundations, the monthly mean temperature of the building mu. be maintained at a minimum of _____.

    A. 60°F
    B. 64°F
    C. 68°F
    D. 70°F

16. A dwelling located in an area with an air freezing index of 3,500 is constructed with a frost-protected shallow foundation. The minimum required horizontal insulation R-value at the corners of the foundation is _____.

    A. 8.0
    B. 8.6
    C. 11.2
    D. 13.1

17. A 9-foot-high plain masonry foundation wall is subjected to 7 feet of unbalanced backfill. If the soil class is GC, the minimum required nominal wall thickness is _____.

    A. 8 inches solid
    B. 10 inches grout
    C. 12 inches solid
    D. 12 inches grout

18. An 8-foot-high, flat concrete foundation wall of nominal 10-inch thickness is subjected to 6 feet of unbalanced backfill. If the soil class is GP, the minimum vertical reinforcement required is _____.

    A. #4 at 38 inches on center
    B. #5 at 47 inches on center
    C. #6 at 43 inches on center
    D. No vertical reinforcement required

19. Where masonry veneer is used, concrete and masonry foundations shall extend a minimum of _____ inches above adjacent finished grade.

    A. 4
    B. 6
    C. 8
    D. 12

20. Where the foundation wall supports a minimum of _____ feet of unbalanced backfill, backfill shall not be placed against the wall until the wall has sufficient strength and has been anchored to the floor above or has been sufficiently braced.

    A. 2
    B. 4
    C. 6
    D. 8

21. Where wood studs having an Fb value of 1320 are used in a wood foundation wall, the minimum stud size shall be _____ and the maximum stud spacing shall be _____ on center.

    A. 2 inches by 4 inches, 24 inches
    B. 2 inches by 4 inches, 16 inches
    C. 2 inches by 6 inches, 24 inches
    D. 2 inches by 6 inches, 16 inches

22. The maximum height of backfill permitted against a wood foundation wall not designed by AWC PWF?

    A. 3 feet
    B. 4 feet
    C. 6 feet
    D. 7 feet

23. Required foundation drains of gravel or crushed stone shall extend a minimum of _____ inches beyond the outside edge of the footing and _____ inches above the top of the footing.

    A. 6, 4
    B. 6, 6
    C. 12, 4
    D. 12, 6

24. As a general rule, the under-floor space between the bottom of floor joists and the earth shall be provided with ventilation openings sized for a minimum net area of 1 square foot for each _____ square feet of under-floor area.

A. 100
B. 120
C. 150
D. 200

25. Access to an under-floor space through a perimeter wall shall be provided by a minimum _____ access opening.

    A. 16-inch-by-20-inch
    B. 16-inch-by-24-inch
    C. 18-inch-by-24-inch
    D. 18-inch-by-30-inch

26. Frost protection is not required for a foundation that supports a freestanding accessory structure of light-framed construction that has a maximum floor area of _____ square feet and a maximum eave height of _____ feet.

    A. 200, 10
    B. 400, 10
    C. 400, 12
    D. 600, 10

27. Gravel used as a footing material for a wood foundation shall be washed, well graded and have a maximum stone size of _____ inch.

    A. ¼
    B. ½
    C. ¾
    D. 1

28. Horizontal insulation used in a frost protected shallow foundation system shall be protected against damage if it is located less than _____ inches below the ground surface.

    A. 12
    B. 15
    C. 18
    D. 24

29. Where waterproofing of a masonry foundation wall is necessary due to the presence of a high-water table, a minimum membrane thickness of _____-mil is required if the waterproofing material is polymer-modified asphalt.

    A. 6
    B. 30
    C. 40
    D. 60

30. Ventilating openings providing under-floor ventilation shall be located so that at least one such open is installed a maximum of _____ feet from each corner of the building.

A. 2
B. 3
C. 5
D. 6

31. A minimum of _____ anchor bolt(s) located in the _____ of the plate section is required to anchor maximum 24-inch-long walls connecting offset braced wall panels.

    A. 1, center third
    B. 1, within the middle one-half
    C. 2, outer one-fourths
    D. 2, within 6 inches of each end

32. Unless specifically approved, the maximum slump permitted for concrete placed in removable foundation wall forms is _____ inches.

    A. 4
    B. 4 ½
    C. 5
    D. 6

33. Where one coat of complying surface-bonding cement is used as the required dampproofing over the parging of a masonry foundation wall, the cement coating must be a minimum of _____ inch thick.

    A. 1/8
    B. 3/16
    C. ¼
    D. 3/8

34. Steel columns used as a part of a foundation system shall be a minimum of _____ inches in diameter standard pipe size or approved equivalent.

    A. 3
    B. 3 ½
    C. 4
    D. 5

35. The continuous vapor barrier required in an unvented crawl space shall extend a minimum of _____ inches up the stem wall.

    A. 3
    B. 4
    C. 6
    D. 8

Please see Answer Key on the following page

4/6/23

International Residential Code, 2021
Chapter 4 – Questions and Answers
Answer Key

	Answer	**Section #**
1.	B	401.3
2.	B	Table 401.4.1 Presumptive Load-Bearing Values of Foundation Materials
3.	C	Table 402.2 Minimum Specified Compressive Strength of Concrete
4.	C	Table 402.2 Minimum Specified Compressive Strength of Concrete Note d
5.	A	Table 403.1(1) Minimum Width and Thickness for Concrete Footings for Light Frame Construction
6.	D	408.6
7.	B	403.1.1
8.	B	Figure 403.1(2) Permanent Wood Foundation Basement Wall Section
9.	A	403.1.3.1
10.	D	403.1.4
11.	B	403.1.5
12.	C	403.1.6
13.	A	403.1.6
14.	B	Table 405.1 Properties of Soils Classified According to the Unified Soil Classification System
15.	B	403.3
16.	C	Table 403.3(1) Minimum Footing Depth and Insulation Requirements for Frost-Protected Footings in Heated Buildings
17.	B	404.1.l(1) Plain Masonry Foundation Walls
18.	D	404.1.2(4) Minimum Vertical Reinforcement For 10-Inch Nominal Flat Concrete Basement Walls
19.	A	404.1.6
20.	B	404.1.7, Exception
21.	D	404.2.2
22.	B	404.2.3
23.	D	405.1
24.	C	408.2
25.	B	408.4
26.	D	403.1.4.1, Exception 1
27.	C	403.2
28.	A	403.3.2
29.	C	406.2
30.	B	408.2
31.	A	403.1.6, Exception 1
32.	D	404.1.3.3.4
33.	A	406.1
34.	A	407.3
35.	C	408.3

International Residential Code, 2021
Chapter 5
Questions and Answers

1. A minimum design live load of _____ psf shall be used for the determination of the maximum allowable floor joist spans in attics that are accessed by a fixed stairway.

   A. 10
   B. 20
   C. 30
   D. 40

2. Where 2-inch by 10-inch floor joists of #2 hem-fir are spaced at 16 inches on center, the maximum allowable span where such joists support a sleeping room and a dead load of 10 psf is _____.

   A. 16 feet, 0 inches
   B. 16 feet, 10 inches
   C. 17 feet, 8 inches
   D. 19 feet, 8 inches

3. Where 2-inch by 10-inch floor joists of #1 spruce-pine-fir are spaced at 16 inches on center, the maximum allowable span where such joists support a living room and a dead load of 20 psf is _____.

   A. 14 feet, 1 inch
   B. 15 feet, 5 inches
   C. 16 feet, 0 inches
   D. 16 feet, 9 inches

4. Where the ground snow load is 30 psf, what is the maximum allowable span of a built-up spruce-pine-fir girder consisting of three 2 by 12s when it is located at an exterior bearing wall and supports a roof, a ceiling and one center-bearing floor in a building having a width of 24 feet?

   A. 6 feet, 2 inches
   B. 7 feet, 2 inches
   C. 7 feet, 5 inches
   D. 8 feet, 5 inches

5. Where a built-up girder of three Southern pine 2 by 10s is used for an exterior bearing wall, what is the minimum number of jack studs required to support a girder that carries a roof, ceiling and one clear span floor in a building having a width of 12 feet?

    A. 1
    B. 2
    C. 3
    D. 4

6. What is the maximum allowable girder span for an interior bearing wall using a built-up girder consisting of three hem fir 2 by 10s and supporting one floor in a building having a width of 36 feet?

    A. 4 feet, 6 inches
    B. 6 feet, 7 inches
    C. 8 feet, 1 inch
    D. 11 feet, 5 inches

7. Doubled joists under parallel bearing partitions that are separated to permit the installation of piping or vents shall be blocked at maximum intervals of _____ feet on center.

    A. 3
    B. 2.5
    C. 4
    D. 5

8. The ends of floor joists shall bear a minimum of _____ inch/inch(es) on wood or metal.

    A. 1
    B. 1 ½
    C. 2 ½
    D. 3

9. Where floor joists frame from opposite sides across the top of a wood girder and are lapped, the minimum lap shall be _____ inches.

    A. 3
    B. 4
    C. 6
    D. 8

10. Bridging shall be provided to support floor joists laterally where the minimum joist depth exceeds _____ nominal size.

    A. 3 inches by 12 inches
    B. 8 inches by 10 inches
    C. 4 inches by 16 inches
    D. 2 inches by 12 inches

11. The maximum permitted length of a notch in a floor joist is _____.

    A. 2 inches
    B. Twice the notch depth
    C. 1/3 the depth of the member
    D. 1/6 the depth of the member

12. A hole bored through a floor joist shall have a maximum diameter of _____ the depth of the member.

    A. 2
    B. 1/6
    C. 1/4
    D. 1/3

13. Where a solid lumber floor joist is both notched and bored, a minimum of _____ inch(es) shall be provided between the notch and the bored hole.

    A. 1
    B. 1 ½
    C. 2
    D. 4

14. Where a ceiling is suspended below the floor framing, draftstops shall be installed so that the maximum area of any concealed space is _____ square feet.

    A. 100
    B. 400
    C. 1,000
    D. 1,500

15. Where wood structural panels are used for required draftstops in concealed floor/ceiling assemblies, the minimum thickness mandated is _____ inch.

    A. 5/16
    B. 3/8
    C. 15/32
    D. 23/32

16. Wood structural panels 15/32-inch thick are to be used as subfloor sheathing and are to be covered with 3/4-inch wood finish flooring installed at right angles to the joists. The maximum allowable span of the wood structural panels if the span rating of the panels is 32/16 is _____ inches.

    A. 0; the panels may not be used as subfloor sheathing
    B. 16
    C. 20
    D. 24

17. Where Species Group 2 sanded plywood is used as combination subfloor underlayment, the minimum required plywood thickness where the joists are spaced at 16 inches on center is _____ inch.

    A. ½
    B. 5/8
    C. ¾
    D. 7/8

18. Steel floor framing constructed in accordance with the prescriptive provisions of the IRC is limited to buildings a maximum of _____ stories above grade plane with each story having a maximum length perpendicular to the joist span of _____ feet.

    A. 2, 40
    B. 2, 60
    C. 3, 40
    D. 3, 60

19. Screws attaching floor sheathing to cold-formed steel joists shall be installed with a minimum edge distance of _____ inch.

    A. ¼
    B. 3/8
    C. ½
    D. 5/8

20. In a steel floor framing system, No. 8 screws spaced at a maximum of _____ inches on center at the edges and _____ inches on center at the intermediate supports shall be used to fasten the subfloor to the floor joists.

    A. 6, 10
    B. 6, 12
    C. 8, 12
    D. 8, 14

21. Cold-formed 33 ksi steel joists are installed as single spans at 16 inches on center in the floor framing system for a dwelling. If the nominal joist size is 800S162-43, the maximum span for a 40 psf live load is _____.

    A. 10 feet, 4 inches
    B. 12 feet, 0 inches
    C. 13 feet, 5 inches
    D. 14 feet, 10 inches

22. Where a wood beam does not bear directly on a masonry wall, a 2-inch-thick sill plate must be provided under the beam with a minimum nominal bearing area of _____ square inches.

    A. 32
    B. 48
    C. 60
    D. 64

23. The maximum fill depth when preparing a site for construction of a concrete slab-on-ground floor _____ inches is for earth and _____ inches for clean sand or gravel.

    A. 6, 12
    B. 8, 16
    C. 8, 24
    D. 12, 24

24. A base course is not required for the prepared subgrade for a concrete floor slab below grade where the soil is classified as _____.

    A. GM
    B. SC
    C. CH
    D. OH

25. Where a vapor retarder is required between a concrete floor slab and the prepared subgrade, the joints of the vapor retarder shall be lapped a minimum of _____ inches.

    A. 2
    B. 4
    C. 6
    D. 8

26. Where supporting only a light-frame exterior bearing wall and roof, the maximum cantilever span for 2 by 10 floor joists spaced at 16 inches on center, provided the roof has a width of 32 feet and the ground snow load is 30 psf is _____ inches.

    A. 18
    B. 21
    C. 22
    D. 26

27. Where supporting an exterior balcony in an area having a ground snow load of 50 psf, the maximum cantilever span for 2 x 12 floor joists spaced at 16 inches on center is _____ inches.

    A. 49
    B. 57
    C. 67
    D. 72

28. Unless the joists are of sufficient size to carry the load, bearing partitions perpendicular to floor joists shall be offset a maximum of _____ from supporting girders, walls or partitions.

    A. 6 inches
    B. 12 inches
    C. The depth of the floor sheathing
    D. The depth of the floor joists

29. Where an opening in floor framing is framed with a single header joist the same size as the floor joist, the maximum header joist span shall be _____ feet.

    A. 3
    B. 4
    C. 6
    D. 12

30. If a base course is required for a concrete floor slab installed below grade, the minimum thickness of base course shall be _____ inches.

    A. 3
    B. 4
    C. 6
    D. 8

31. Unless supported by other approved means, the ends of each joist, beam or girder shall have a minimum of _____ inches of bearing on masonry or concrete.

    A. 1 ½
    B. 2
    C. 3
    D. 4

32. Notches at the ends of solid lumber joists, rafters and beams shall have a maximum depth of
    _____.

    A. 2 inches
    B. 3 inches
    C. One-half the depth of the member
    D. One-fourth the depth of the member

33. Holes bored into solid lumber joists, rafter and beams shall be located a minimum of _____ from the top or bottom of the member.

    A. 1 inch
    B. 2 inches
    C. One-sixth the member depth
    D. One-third the member depth

34. The ends of deck joists shall have not less than _____ inches of bearing on wood or metal and not less than _____ inches of bearing on concrete or masonry over its entire width.

    A. 1; 3
    B. 1 ½; 3
    C. 2; 3
    D. 2; 4

35. Where reinforcement is provided in concrete slab-on-ground floors, the reinforcement shall be supported to remain within the _____ of the slab during the concrete placement.

    A. Middle one-third
    B. Middle one-half
    C. Center to the upper one-third
    D. Center to the upper one-fourth

Please see Answer Key on the following page

ABC 08/20/2021

	Answer	**Section #**
1.	C	502.3.1
2.	B	Table R502.3.1(1) Floor Joist Spans for Common Lumber Species (Residential sleeping areas, live load = 30 psf, L/Δ = 360)
3.	A	Table R502.3.1(2) Floor Joist Spans for Common Lumber Species (Residential live load = 40 psf, L/Δ = 360)
4.	D	502.5
		Table R602.7(1) Girder Spans and Header Spans for Exterior Bearing Walls
5.	B	502.5
		Table R602.7(1) Girder Spans and Header Spans for Exterior Bearing Walls
6.	B	502.5
		Table 602.7(2) Girder Spans and Header Spans for Interior Bearing Walls
7.	C	502.4
8.	B	502.6
9.	A	502.6.1
10.	D	502.7.1
11.	C	502.8.1
12.	D	502.8.1
13.	C	502.8.1
14.	C	502.12, 302.12
15.	B	502.12, 302.12.1
16.	D	Table 503.2.1.1(1), Allowable Spans and Loads for Wood Structural Panels for Roof and Subfloor Sheathing and Combination Subfloor Underlayment (Note I
17.	B	Table 503.2.1.1(2) Allowable Spans for Sanded Plywood Combination Subfloc Underlayment
18.	D	505.1.1
19.	B	505.2.5
20.	B	Table 505.3.1(2) Floor Fastening Schedule
21.	C	Table 505.3.2 Allowable Spans for Cold-Formed Steel Joists—Single or Continuous Spans
22.	B	502.6
23.	C	506.2.1
24.	A	506.2.2, Exception; Table 405.1
25.	C	506.2.3
26.	A	Table 502.3.3(1) Cantilever Spans for Floor Joists Supporting Light-Frame Exterior Bearing Wall and Roof Only
27.	C	Table 502.3.3(2) Cantilever Spans for Floor Joists Supporting Exterior Balcon
28.	D	502.4
29.	B	502.10

	Answer	Section #
30.	B	506.2.2
31.	C	502.6
32.	D	502.8.1
33.	B	502.8.1
34.	B	507.6.1
35.	C	506.2.4

International Residential Code, 2021
Chapter 6 and 7
Questions and Answers

1. The maximum center-to-center stud spacing permitted for a 2-inch by 6-inch, 8-foot-high wood stud bearing wall supporting two floors, roof and ceiling is _____ inches.

    A. 8
    B. 12
    C. 16
    D. 24

2. In wood wall framing where top and bottom plates are attached to the studs, which of the following fastening methods is acceptable?

    A. 3-8d box, toe nailed
    B. 3-8d common, end nailed
    C. 3-10d box, toe nailed
    D. 3-10d box, end nailed

3. The minimum offset for end joints in a double top plate shall be _____ inches.

    A. 24
    B. 36
    C. 48
    D. 60

4. A single top plate is permitted in a wood stud bearing wall where the rafters or joists are located with _____ of the center of the studs.

    A. 0 inches; no tolerance is permitted
    B. 1 inch
    C. 1 ½ inches
    D. 5 inches

5. Where the wall sheathing is used to resist wind pressures, the maximum stud spacing permitted for 3 inch wood structural panel wall sheathing with a span rating of 24/0 is _____ inches o.c.

    A. 12
    B. 16
    C. 20
    D. 24

6. In a nonbearing partition, a wood stud may be notched a maximum of _____ inch

   A. 5/8 inch
   B. 1 3/8 inches
   C. 40 percent of the stud width
   D. 60 percent of the stud width

7. A bored hole shall be located a minimum of _____ inch from the edge of a wood stud.

   A. 3/
   B. ½
   C. 5/8
   D. 1

8. In a nonbearing interior partition, the maximum diameter permitted for a bored hole in a wood stud is _____.

   A. 1 ½ inches
   B. 25 percent of the stud depth
   C. 40 percent of the stud depth
   D. 60 percent of the stud depth

9. A 15-inch-deep box header in an exterior wall is constructed with wood structural panels on both sides. The maximum allowable header span for a condition where the header supports a clear-span roof truss with a span of 26 feet is _____ feet.

   A. 4
   B. 5
   C. 7
   D. 8

10. _____ is not specifically identified by the IRC as a fireblocking material.

    A. 1/4-inch cement-based millboard
    B. 1/2-inch gypsum board
    C. 15/32-inch wood structural panel
    D. 3/4-inch particleboard

11. Where unfaced fiberglass batt insulation is used as a fireblocking material in the wall cavity of a wood stud wall system, the insulation shall be installed with a minimum vertical height of _____.

    A. 16 inches
    B. 3 feet
    C. 4 feet
    D. The entire stud space

12. A foundation cripple wall shall be considered an additional story for stud sizing requirements where the wall height exceeds _____ feet.

    A. 1.5
    B. 2.5
    C. 3
    D. 4

13. The distance between adjacent edges of braced wall panels along a braced wall line must be a maximum of _____ feet.

    A. 16
    B. 20
    C. 25
    D. 35

14. Where located in Seismic Design Category B, braced wall panels shall begin a maximum of _____ from each end of a braced wall line.

    A. 4
    B. 8
    C. 10
    D. 12 ½

15. Screws for attaching structural sheathing to cold-formed steel wall framing shall have a minimum head diameter of 0.292 inch with countersunk heads and shall be installed with a minimum edge distance of _____ inch.

    A. 1/2
    B. 3/8
    C. 1/4
    D. 3/4

16. When anchor bolts are used to anchor cold-formed steel walls to foundations or floors, the bolts shall extend not less than _____ inches into masonry and _____ inches into concrete.

    A. 7; 6
    B. 10; 6
    C. 14; 7
    D. 15; 7

17. Exterior walls parallel to a braced wall line are permitted to be offset a maximum of _____ feet from the designated braced wall line location.

    A. 2
    B. 4
    C. 5
    D. 6

18. Where ledgers are used at the connection between a masonry wall and a wood floor system having floor joists spanning 16 feet, 1 / 2-inch ledger bolts shall be located at a maximum of _____ on center, provided the building is in Seismic Design Category A, B or C and the wind loads are less than 30 psf.

    A. 1 foot, 0 inches
    B. 1 foot, 3 inches
    C. 1 foot, 9 inches
    D. 2 feet, 0 inches

19. When 1/2-inch gypsum board is used as an interior wall covering and installed perpendicular to framing members at 16 inches on center, the maximum spacing of nails is _____ inches on center where adhesive is used.

    A. 7
    B. 8
    C. 12
    D. 16

20. Screws for attaching gypsum board to wood framing shall penetrate the wood a minimum of _____ inch.

    A. ¼
    B. 3/8
    C. ½
    D. 5/8

21. Water-resistant gypsum board shall not be installed over which of the following classifications of vapor retarders when located in a tub or shower compartment?

    A. I or II
    B. II or III
    C. I, II or III
    D. III only

22. Where 3/8-inch particleboard is used as an exterior wall covering, what type of fasteners are required if the particleboard is attached directly to the studs?

    A. 0.120 nail, 2 inches long
    B. 6d box nail
    C. 8d box nail
    D. Direct attachment to the studs is prohibited

23. In Seismic Design Category D1, metal ties for anchoring masonry veneer to a supporting wall shall support a maximum of _____ square feet of wall area.

    A. 2
    B. 2 2/3
    C. 3 ½
    D. 4 ½

24. An Exterior Insulation Finish System (EIFS) shall terminate a minimum of _____ inch(es) above the finished ground level.

    A. 1
    B. 2
    C. 6
    D. 8

25. The minimum required size of a steel angle spanning 8 feet used as a lintel supporting one story of masonry veneer above is _____.

    A. 3 x 3 x ¼
    B. 4 x 3 x ¼
    C. 5 x 3 ½ x 5/16
    D. 6 x 3 ½ x 5 /16

26. Utility grade studs, where used in loadbearing walls supporting only a roof and a ceiling, shall have a maximum height of _____ feet.

    A. 8
    B. 10
    C. 12
    D. 14

27. Asphalt felt applied as a portion of the exterior wall envelope shall be applied horizontally, with the upper layer lapped over the lower layer a minimum of _____ inch(es).

    A. 1
    B. 2
    C. 4
    D. 6

28. 23/32-inch wood structural panels attached to wall framing with 15 gage staples shall be fastened at a maximum of _____ inches at the panel edges and _____ inches at the intermediate suppo

    A. 3, 6
    B. 4, 8
    C. 5, 10
    D. 6, 12

29. Where the top plate of an interior load-bearing wall is notched by more than _____ percent of i width to accommodate piping, a complying metal tie shall be installed.

    A. 25
    B. 33 1/3
    C. 40
    D. 50

30. A weep screed installed on exterior stud walls in an exterior plaster application must be placed a minimum of _____ inch(es) above paved areas.

    A. 1
    B. 2
    C. 4
    D. 6

31. Where an exterior wall top plate is notched to the extent that a metal tie is required across the opening, the tie shall be fastened to the plate at each side of the opening with a minimum of _____ 10d nails at each side, or equivalent.

    A. Two
    B. Four
    C. Six
    D. Eight

32. For a building located in Seismic Design Category D_0, plate washers used in the connection of braced wall line sills to a concrete foundation shall be a minimum of _____ in size.

    A. 0.188 inch by 2 inches by 2 inches
    B. 0.229 inch by 2 inches by 2 inches
    C. 0.229 inch by 3 inches by 3 inches
    D. 0.375 inch by 3 inches by 3 inches

33. Fasteners for hardboard panel and lap siding shall penetrate a minimum of _____ inch(es) into framing.

    A. ¾
    B. 7/8
    C. 1 ¼
    D. 1 ½

34. End-jointed lumber used in an assembly required by the IRC to have a fire resistance rating must have the designation _____ included in its grade mark.

    A. Fire Assembly Certified (FAC)
    B. Fire Resistant Rated (FRR)
    C. Heat and Fire Resistant (HFR)
    D. Heat Resistant Adhesive (HRA)

35. The water-resistive vapor permeable barrier required to be applied over wood-based wall sheathing shall have a performance level equivalent to that of _____ layer(s) of Grade _____ paper.

    A. One, A
    B. One, B
    C. Two, C
    D. Two, D

Please see Answer Key on the following page

	Answer	**Section #**
1.	C	Table 602.3(5) Size, Height and Spacing of Wood Studs
2.	D	Table 602.3(1), Fastening Schedule #17
3.	A	602.3.2
4.	B	602.3.2, Exception, #2
5.	B	Table 602.3(3) Requirements for Wood Structural Panel Wall Sheathing Used Resist Wind Pressures
6.	C	602.6
7.	C	602.6
8.	D	602.6
9.	D	Table 602.7.3 Maximum Spans for Wood Structural Panel Box Headers
10.	C	602.8, 302.11.1
11.	A	602.8, 302.11.1.2
12.	D	602.9
13.	B	602.10.2.2
14.	C	602.10.2.2
15.	B	603.2.5
16.	D	603.3.1
17.	B	602.10.1.2
18.	A	Figure 606.11(l) Anchorage Requirements for Masonry Walls Located in Seisr Design Category A, B or C and Where Wind Loads Are Less Than 30 Psf
19.	D	Table 702.3.5 Minimum Thickness and Application of Gypsum Board and Gypsum Panel Products
20.	D	702.3.5.1
21.	A	702.3.7
22.	D	Table 703.3(1) Siding Minimum Attachment and Minimum Thickness
23.	A	703.8.4.1, Exception
24.	C	703.9.1
25.	C	Table 703.8.3.1 Allowable Spans for Lintels Supporting Masonry Veneer
26.	A	602.3.1, Exception 1
27.	B	703.2
28.	B	Table 602.3(2) Alternate Attachments to Table R602.3(1)
29.	D	602.6.1
30.	B	703.7.2.1
31.	D	602.6.1
32.	C	602.11.1
33.	D	703.3.4
34.	D	602.1.2
35.	D	703.7.3.1

International Residential Code, 2021
Chapter 8 and 9
Questions and Answers

1. On a site having expansive soil, roof drainage water shall discharge a minimum of _____ feet from the foundation walls or to an approved drainage system.

   A. 2
   B. 5
   C. 4
   D. 10

2. Where the roof pitch is less than _____, the structural members that support rafters and ceiling joists (such as ridge beams, hips and valleys) shall be designed as beams.

   A. 3:12
   B. 4:12
   C. 5:12
   D. 6:12

3. The maximum spacing of collar ties shall be _____ feet on center.

   A. 6
   B. 4
   C. 5
   D. 8

4. Ends of ceiling joists shall be lapped a minimum of _____ inches unless butted and toenailed to the supporting member.

   A. 1 ½
   B. 3
   C. 4
   D. 6

5. Where SPF #2 ceiling joists create an uninhabitable attic without storage and are spaced 24 inches on center, the maximum allowable span when 2-inch by 6-inch members are used is _____.

   A. 11 feet, 2 inches
   B. 14 feet, 5 inches
   C. 14 feet, 9 inches
   D. 15 feet, 11 inches

6. A roof system is subjected to a 50 psf ground snow load and creates a dead load of 20 psf. The ceiling not attached to the rafters. Assuming that rafter ties are provided at the top plate line, the maximum span of 2-inch by 8-inch Hem-Fir#1 rafters spaced at 24 inches on center is _____.

    A. 9 feet, 10 inches
    B. 10 feet, 6 inches
    C. 11 feet, 6 inches
    D. 11 feet, 10 inches

7. Purlins shall be supported by braces having a maximum unbraced length of _____ feet and spaced at a maximum of _____ feet on center.

    A. 8; 4
    B. 8; 6
    C. 12; 4
    D. 12; 6

8. The ends of a ceiling joist shall have a minimum of _____ inches bearing on wood and metal and a minimum of _____ inches on masonry or concrete.

    A. 1 ½; 1 ½
    B. 1 ½; 3
    C. 3; 1 ½
    D. 3; 3

9. Notches in solid sawn lumber ceiling joists shall not be located in the middle _____ of the span and are limited in depth to _____ the depth of the joist.

    A. one-fourth; one-sixth
    B. one-fourth; one-third
    C. one-third; one-sixth
    D. one-third; one-third

10. An opening in a wood framed roof system may be framed with a single header and single trimmer joist provided the header joist is located a maximum of _____ feet from the trimmer joist bearing.

    A. 3
    B. 4
    C. 6
    D. 12

11. Where 15/32-inch wood structural panels having a span rating of 32/16 are used as roof sheathing, the maximum span without edge support is _____ inches.

    A. 16
    B. 24
    C. 28
    D. 32

12. A dwelling is located in an area having a 115 mph wind speed and Exposure B. The ground snow load is 20 psf. What is the maximum allowable rafter span for 800S162-43 50 ksi steel rafters installed at 24 inches on center with a roof slope of 12:12?

    A. 7 feet, 11 inches
    B. 9 feet, 9 inches
    C. 10 feet, 10 inches
    D. 16 feet

13. In a steel-framed roof system, eave overhangs shall not exceed _____ inches in horizontal projection.

    A. 12
    B. 18
    C. 24
    D. 30

14. Openings provided for roof ventilation, where covered with corrosion-resistant wire cloth screening, shall have openings a minimum of _____ inch and a maximum of _____ inch.

    A. 1/16; ¼
    B. 1/8; ¼
    C. ¼; 3/8
    D. ¼; ½

15. A required attic access opening shall have a minimum rough opening size of _____.

    A. 18 inches by 24 inches
    B. 18 inches by 30 inches
    C. 22 inches by 30 inches
    D. 24 inches by 36 inches

16. A net free cross-ventilating area of 1/300 is permitted for roof ventilation in buildings in Climate Zones 6, 7 and 8, provided a minimum _____ vapor barrier is installed on the warm-in-winter side of the ceiling.

    A. Class I only
    B. Class II only
    C. Class III only
    D. Class I or II

17. Fire-retardant-treated wood, when used in roof construction, shall have a maximum listed flame spread index of _____.

    A. 25
    B. 75
    C. 100
    D. 200

18. In the attachment of asphalt shingles, special methods of fastening as established by the manufacturer are required where the roof slope of _____ is exceeded.

    A. 12 units vertical in 12 units horizontal
    B. 15 units vertical in 12 units horizontal
    C. 18 units vertical in 12 units horizontal
    D. 21 units vertical in 12 units horizontal

19. Double underlayment is required for an asphalt shingle application where the roof has a slope of up to _____.

    A. 2:12
    B. 2 ½:12
    C. 3:12
    D. 4:12

20. In an asphalt shingle roof application, step flashing on a sidewall shall be a minimum of _____ inches high and _____ inches wide.

    A. 3, 6
    B. 4, 4
    C. 6, 6
    D. 6, 8

21. Nails used to attach concrete roof tiles to the roof deck shall penetrate the deck a minimum of _____ inch or through the thickness of the deck, whichever is less.

    A. ½
    B. 5/8
    C. ¾
    D. 7/8

22. Where the cantilevered portion of a rafter is notched, a minimum of _____ inches of the member depth must remain.

    A. 3
    B. 3 ½
    C. 4
    D. 5

23. Where No. 2 wood shingles of naturally durable wood are installed on a roof having a 5:12 pitch, the maximum weather exposure for 16-inch shingles shall be _____ inches.

    A. 3 ½
    B. 4
    C. 5 ½
    D. 6 ½

24. For preservative-treated tapersawn shakes installed on a roof, the spacing between wood shakes shall be a minimum of _____ inch and a maximum of _____ inch.

    A. 1/8; 3/8
    B. 1/8; 5/8
    C. ¼; 3/8
    D. 3/8; 5/8

25. For a wood shake roof system, sheet metal roof valley flashing shall extend a minimum of _____ inches from the centerline of the valley in each direction.

    A. 4
    B. 7
    C. 11
    D. 12

26. A notch located in the end of a solid lumber ceiling joist shall have a maximum depth of _____.

    A. 1 inch
    B. 2 inches
    C. one-third the depth of the member
    D. one-fourth the depth of the member

27. In the framing of an opening in ceiling construction, approved hangers are not required for the header joist to trimmer joist connections where the header joist span is a maximum of _____ feet.

    A. 4
    B. 6
    C. 8
    D. 12

28. Where eave or cornice vents are installed, a minimum _____-inch air space shall be provided between the insulation and the roof sheathing at the vent location.

    A. ½
    B. 1
    C. 2
    D. 3

29. Where the attic height is 30 inches or greater, an access opening is not required in attics of combustible construction where the attic space is a maximum of _____ square feet in area.

    A. 30
    B. 50
    C. 100
    D. 120

30. Overflow scuppers utilized for secondary roof drainage shall have a minimum size _____ of th roof drain.

    A. equal to that
    B. twice the size
    C. three times the size
    D. four times the size

31. A ridge board shall be a minimum of _____ -inch in nominal thickness and have a minimum depth equal to _____ .

    A. 1, the cut end of the rafter
    B. 1, the nominal depth of the rafter
    C. 2, the actual depth of the rafter
    D. 2, the cut end of the rafter

32. The minimum total net free ventilating area required for a 1,500-square-foot attic space where 75 percent of the required ventilation area is provided by ventilators located in the upper portion of the a space is _____ square feet.

    A. 5
    B. 7.5
    C. 10
    D. 15

33. Where an unvented conditioned attic assembly is utilized for a residence, the use of wood shakes on t roof would require a minimum continuous _____ -inch vented air space between the shakes the roofing felt.

    A. ¼
    B. ½
    C. ¾
    D. 1

34. Where required on an asphalt-shingled roof of 5:12 slope, an ice barrier shall extend from the lowest edges of the roof surfaces to a minimum of _____ inches inside the exterior wall line of the building.

    A. 8
    B. 12
    C. 16
    D. 24

35. Drip edges provided at eaves and gables of asphalt shingle roofs shall extend a minimum of
_____ inch below the roof sheathing.

    A. ¼
    B. ½
    C. ¾
    D. 1

Please see Answer Key on the following page

International Residential Code, 2021
Chapter 8 and 9
Questions and Answers
Answer Key

	Answer	**Section #**
1.	B	801.3
2.	A	802.4.4
3.	B	802.4.6
4.	B	802.5.2.1
5.	C	Table 802.5.1(1) Ceiling Joist Spans for Common Lumber Species
6.	A	Table 802.4.1(5) Rafter Spans for Common Lumber Species
7.	A	802.4.5
8.	B	802.6
9.	C	802.7.1, 502.8.1
10.	A	802.9
11.	C	803.2.2
		Table 503.2.1.1(1) Allowable Spans and Loads For Wood Structural Panels For Roof and Subfloor Sheathing And Combination Subfloor Underlayment
12.	D	Table 804.3.2.1(2) Ultimate Design Wind Speed to Equivalent Snow Load Conversion
		Table 804.3.2.1(1) Roof Rafter Spans
13.	C	804.3.2.1.1
14.	A	806.1
15.	C	807.1
16.	D	806.2, Exception, #1
17.	A	802.1.5
18.	D	905.2.6
19.	D	905.1.1
		Table 905.1.1(2) Underlayment Application
20.	B	905.2.8.3
21.	C	905.3.6
22.	B	802.7.1.1
23.	B	Table 905.7.5(1) Wood Shingle Weather Exposure and Roof Slope
24.	D	905.8.6
25.	C	905.8.8
26.	D	802.7.1, 502.8.1
27.	B	802.9
28.	B	806.3
29.	A	807.1
30.	C	903.4.1
31.	A	802.3
32.	C	806.2
		$1,500 \div 150 = 10$

Answer	Section #
A	806.5
D	905.2.7
	905.1.2
A	905.2.8.5

Made in the USA
Columbia, SC
12 August 2024